ROUTLEDGE LIBRARY EDITIONS:
ORGANIZATIONS: THEORY & BEHAVIOUR

THE SOCIOLOGY OF WORK

THE SOCIOLOGY OF WORK
A Critical Annotated Bibliography

PARVIN GHORAYSHI

Volume 16

Routledge
Taylor & Francis Group

LONDON AND NEW YORK

First published in 1990

This edition first published in 2013
by Routledge
2 Park Square, Milton Park, Abingdon, Oxon, OX14 4RN

Simultaneously published in the USA and Canada
by Routledge
711 Third Avenue, New York, NY 10017

Routledge is an imprint of the Taylor & Francis Group, an informa business

© 1990 Parvin Ghorayshi

British Library Cataloguing in Publication Data
A catalogue record for this book is available from the British Library

ISBN: 978-0-415-65793-8 (Set)
eISBN: 978-0-203-38369-8 (Set)
ISBN: 978-0-415-82264-0 (Volume 16)
eISBN: 978-0-203-37045-2 (Volume 16)

Publisher's Note
The publisher has gone to great lengths to ensure the quality of this reprint but points out that some imperfections in the original copies may be apparent.

Disclaimer
The publisher has made every effort to trace copyright holders and would welcome correspondence from those they have been unable to trace.

Printed and bound by CPI Group (UK) Ltd, Croydon, CR0 4YY

THE SOCIOLOGY OF WORK
A Critical Annotated Bibliography

Parvin Ghorayshi

GARLAND PUBLISHING, INC. • NEW YORK & LONDON
1990

Library of Congress Cataloging-in-Publication Data

Ghorayshi, Parvin.
   The sociology of work: a critical annotated bibliography / Parvin
Ghorayshi.
      p.   cm. — (Garland library of sociology; vol. 17) (Garland
reference library of social science; vol. 591)
   ISBN 0–8240–3438–4 (alk. paper)
   1. Industrial sociology—Bibliography. 2. Work—Bibliography.
I. Title. II. Series. III. Series: Garland reference library of
social science; v. 591.
Z7164.I45G46   1990
[HD6955]
016.3063'6—dc20   90–2840
                                           CIP

Printed on acid-free, 250-year-life paper
Manufactured in the United States of America

To my mother,
to the memory of my father
and grandparents

CONTENTS

Experience of unemployment
Personal and social cost of unemployment—Policy issues

Work-related diseases, injuries and accidents—Types of work
   hazards—Workers' response
Unions' response—Workers' compensation—Social and personal
   costs—Prevention and safety programs

New challenges facing unions
Union membership
Union's power
Gender, race, ethnicity and unions—Government and unions
White collar unionism
Unions and the changing global economy

Workers' participation in decision-making
Types of enterprise democratization
Examples of democratic organizations
The future of participatory democracy at work

Contents

PREFACE OF THE GENERAL EDITOR

The twentieth century has experienced a major transformation in the workplace. While the nature of work has evolved only gradually, the character of the labor force has changed at a much faster rate. The rise in the educational attainment of workers, the changing structure of the family, and greater affluence among workers demand more sensitivity and careful attention by management to the concerns of their workers. The traditional nine-to-five work patterns have been undergoing significant changes. In the past few years, flexitime, job-sharing, permanent part-time employment, a compressed work week, telecommuting, telework or location independent work, and alternative workstyles of single parents have provided a variety of options for employees and employers.

Micro-electronics technology poses a special threat to the growing educated workforce. The same technologies that are eliminating many jobs are also creating lots of new ones. But workers need to be retrained if they are to be able to fill the new jobs. The proliferation of personal computers has facilitated a shift toward more part-time and home-based work. Changing values are changing the face of the workplace as workers demand meaningful participation in decision-making.

In the twenty-first century, dramatic changes will occur in employment patterns. These changes are going to affect how we work and how we are educated and trained for jobs. Much of the work in the next century, it is predicted, will be done by teleworkers—people who stay at home and commute to work via telecommunications. Work in the future may be challenging and satisfying, providing you can get it and can do it.

It is projected that in the next century employers will increasingly provide paid "mental health days," or flexible leave time, to allow workers to relieve stress. Stress and mental health care will become more important workplace issues in the future. Furthermore, companies will recognize the need to provide more "elder care" benefits—similar to child-care benefits—to assist workers who must care for older relatives.

In recent years, there has been a tremendous increase in research in the sociology of work and industry. Sociologists, economists, psychologists and other social scientists have focused on work structures such as occupations, industries, classes, organizations and unions and their influence on the organization of work, labor-management relations, labor markets, productivity, earnings inequality, and workers' attitudes and behaviors. The sociology of work has shifted its focus away from its earlier micro concerns, such as work and workers, to macro issues, i.e., studying effects of social structures on individuals. This shift in focus has also changed our conception of the worker from a social into an economic one.

Industrial sociology, from the 1930s to the 1950s, was primarily concerned with human relations in factories and offices, and the cultures and the problems of occupational groups. During the 1960s, the field of industrial sociology focused on workers' values and satisfaction and the impact of technology and bureaucracy on workers. Since the 1970s, however, Marxist perspectives have contributed to new lines of research related to alienation, the labor process, the dual economy and segmented labor markets, and earnings determination.

This reference volume reflects the changing world of work. It includes recent research on the various dimensions of work, such as the structure of the labor force, labor market segmentation, technology, employment/unemployment, trade unions, and industrial democracy. A large number of studies cited in this book indicate that what we are experiencing today is more than a cyclical adjustment and help us encounter issues associated with the complex and changing nature of work. Furthermore, with their critical approach, the annotated citations reveal the problems, such as labor market discrimination, unemployment, health hazards and so on, that workers face.

This book provides an integrated view of the various dimensions of work, its distinguishing characteristics, and issues both peculiar, as well as common, to industrialized countries. The author has attempted to synthesize the growing body of recent research and shows how different disciplines have approached work and industrial relations.

Although a major focus of this book is on Western industrialized countries, it draws numerous examples from other societies and makes clear that, in today's world, it is almost impossible to understand the complexity of the issue in any single nation in isolation from other nations. By adopting an interdisciplinary and interactional perspective, this volume aims to provide both the scholar and the lay reader with a range of approaches and debates that have made a significant contribution toward understanding the changing nature of work and its social impact. It is intended as an introduction but assumes that the reader is not completely unfamiliar with sociological approaches to the study of work. It attempts to set out the background of theory and research with which students need to be familiar in order to undertake more advanced research. Parvin Ghorayshi has done extensive research on work and industrial relations. This book is a continuation of her research interests. The multidisciplinary content and emphasis on sociological works make this reference volume useful to both specialists and non-specialists alike.

DAN A. CHEKKI
University of Winnipeg

ACKNOWLEDGMENTS

I am grateful to Dan Chekki for his generous co-operation. I would like to acknowledge the help that I have received from Laureen Narfason and Kimberley Smyrski. I owe a special debt to Poran Ghorayshi for being always willing to help. I thank Darlene Mann for typing the manuscript. I would like to express my appreciation to SSHRC for providing the financial support for this book.

LIST OF JOURNALS USED

-Acta Sociologica
-American Journal of Sociology
-Canadian Journal of African Studies
-Canadian Public Policy
-Canadian Public Administration
-Economic and Industrial Democracy
-Group and Organizational Studies
-Harvard Business Review
-Industrial and Labor Relations Review
-Industrial Relations
-International Journal of Comparative Studies
-International Labour Review
-International Migration Review
-International Social Science Journal
-International Sociology
-Labor History
-Occupational Health
-Occupational Health and Safety
-Organization Studies
-Radical America
-Relations Industriels
-Review of Radical Political Economy
-Science and Technology and Human Values
-Signs
-Sociological Perspective
-Social Science Quarterly
-Studies in Comparative International Development
-The British Journal of Sociology
-The Canadian Review of Sociology and Anthropology
-The Journal of Developing Areas
-The Sociological Quarterly
-Work and Occupations

INTRODUCTION

This volume on the sociology of work appears when, perhaps more than ever before, problems of work are at the forefront of public consciousness and debate, as well as academic theorizing and research. The question of work has gained a central place in the political and economic debate, especially in the industrialized countries. Structural and technological changes both at national and international levels have raised questions about the structures and processes of our society: What is work? Why and how is it divided up, organized and rewarded? Could it be different?

Over the last decade, the sociology of work has dealt with the most sensitive and important problems of social life. Considerable changes in both the real world of work and the academic analysis on the nature of work have occurred, and this increasingly complex field of study has been covered by many theories and research, gradually building up an impressive body of knowledge. Furthermore, the growth of new intellectual approaches has provided fresh answers to the old questions, and raised novel issues as legitimate areas of investigation. The traditional sociology of work and occupations, written in the 1950's and '60's, began to collapse at the same time these changes were taking place. The old concepts were unable to cope with the growing changes. Clearly, earlier studies on the world of work need to be updated, and more clearly still, they need to be updated in ways that take into account a number of complex social and economic developments, as well as the multi-disciplinary nature of the issue under study.

Growing specialization in sociology, as in other academic disciplines, has produced a variety of sub-areas of study. Thus the area of work has been further divided as scholars have concentrated more closely on issues such as labor history, industrial relations, organizational behavior, occupational change, women's studies, technology and society, quality of work, industrial democracy, alienation, unemployment and occupational health and safety, to mention only some of the more central topics. Such specialization has been essential for the development of the discipline, but it has impeded our ability to develop a broad understanding of the nature of work in contemporary societies.

The sociology of work, like most sociological sub-areas, crosses into related disciplines. In order to understand the complexity of the problems faced in industrial life, we must draw upon diverse literature. The unique feature of this volume is that it brings together some of the most significant achievements from different traditions. It presents students of work with examples of how different disciplinary approaches and different research methods can be used to shed light on the complex nature of work, not just in departments of sociology. This task, however, is not an easy one, since one has to choose from many topics.

In this book, we include those studies that have been relatively well explored by social scientists and give the reader an insight into the complexity of the problems faced in industrial life. Because of the broad scope of the presentation, our coverage of the literature is far from exhaustive. Instead, we selectively discuss the primary literature in such a way that it will highlight the present themes, debates, problems and issues in the sociology of work and industry. The entries were chosen because they make an important contribution to the direction of the sociological observation of work, and are essential for understanding the real world of work today. Special attention is paid to lines of study that reveal new aspects of social processes in industry, and challenge the conventional wisdom of the established lines of thought.

Of course, the need to integrate many different perspectives and approaches into a comprehensive whole poses enormous difficulties. The sociology of work has been affected by the polarization of theoretical positions and research methods, which has resulted in many divergent views on the substance of the world of work. We attempt to make it clear that there is no one best theory to deal with the experience of work, and no universal methodology for its successful exploration.

This volume is intended to be inter-disciplinary with an international dimension. It provides a variety of perspectives for studying the historical, economic, political, social and ideological nature of work. Although the emphasis is on the experience of work in industrialized countries, the entries make it clear that, in today's world, it is impossible to grasp the complexity of work in any single country in isolation from other societies. By adopting this approach, we hope to bring out the interdependence between nations, as well as the similarities and differences that exist among various places and societies regarding work relations and work place activities.

We sought books, articles and reports that, together, would address a broad range of issues, and bring a variety of perspectives to bear on work in contemporary societies--with a focus on western industrialized countries. We were committed to a conception of the book which would not only place work in its social context, but would also provide a dynamic, rather than static, picture--hence the historical and comparative dimension of many of the entries.

This critical annotated bibliography, by relying on primary sources and drawing upon diverse disciplines, provides an introduction to the field of work, and could serve as a research and reference tool for students, researchers, academics, librarians, managers, occupational health professionals, labor activists, unions, and the general public, at all levels, in various sub-areas of the sociology of work. It will help them find their way into the literature on work in pursuit of answers to their questions.

We begin our examination of work by understanding the ideology behind working and the way work is influenced and perceived. It involves much more than employment and income. The type of work individuals perform has a profound impact on their life chances, and it remains a critical factor in defining their existence. This section explores the concept of work, workers' attitudes towards their jobs, and the meaning people attach to their work from various points of view and cultural ideals. The entries provide a fascinating account of the ideas that have been used to legitimize work. We adopt a cross-cultural frame of reference and place work in the context of social relationships and symbolic values. The items looked at bring out the systematic relationship between culture, social and economic institutions, and work.

The following section, **understanding the global context**, brings out the effects of wider economic and social influences on the interaction among workers, employers, unions and the state. It shows there is a wide recognition that a fundamental transformation is taking place in the economic structure on a world scale. We are witnessing a major shift towards the internationalization of capital under the sway of Transnational Corporations and the enhanced mobility of capital and labor, facilitated by modern communication technology. Such a shift implies a transition away from the classic international division of labor towards a restructured world economy, wherein the Third World is increasingly providing sites for industries which manufacture goods for sale on the world economy.

The fact is that the integration of the world economy has eroded the significance of national boundaries, and weakened the ability of either governments or unions, in a single country, to insulate themselves from external influences. The movement towards globalization of production and the creation of a global market poses new questions for our understanding of work in today's society.

In the two sections on work relations and work experiences, it is essentially the social character of work that we seek to describe and explain, bearing in mind that the social pattern of work must be understood in the widest possible sense to include how work is patterned and organized, awarded and evaluated, and controlled. The focus is on work place relations and how they are formally and informally structured, how people relate, and in what way.

The entries bring out the issues of central importance to the labor process debate--power and class--and are concerned with the politics of occupations. They discuss, at some length, the issue of occupational control, skill, and the transformation of the labor process. The intention is simply to understand what goes on at work--the whole complex mesh of the social work process: What are the limits of various forms of organizations, in whose interest are they, and under what circumstances are claims for occupational control likely to be effective? It becomes very clear, in different places and at different times, that workers are neither a homogeneous class united in opposition to management, nor a mass of individuals eager for their own reasons to co-operate, even in limited way, with their bosses.

This leads to a discussion about the nature and characteristics of the labor force, and its future trends. The entries offer a discussion about the ways in which the new occupations associated with the new technology, and the new international division of labor, are likely to emerge. The experiences of various countries are presented to grasp the universal nature of the labor force transformation, as well as the differences. The entries bring out the major labor market changes and trends, the rise of the female labor force participation, the increase in service sector jobs, the occupations associated with the new technology, the growth of two-income families, the growing importance of part-time work, the increasing share of employment in the service sector of the economy, the importance of public sectors, etc. Also discussed are the sociological consequences of this transformation of employment on the nature of work, its class structure, and international labor migration.

After the section on the nature and organization of work, we focus on the divisions and cleavages among workers. The entries on the segmentation of the labor market show that there are persistent and important objective divisions among them. These objective divisions have played a major role in forestalling the efforts of workers to build a unified movement. The key to labor market differentiation is said to lie in the practices and structures beyond the strictly economic sphere, which are found in but not created by, the social relations of production. This case has been argued most forcefully and thoroughly with regard to sexual differentiation in the labor market. A number of other divisions of labor--racial, ethnic--can be regarded as broadly analogous, although less deeply rooted.

The essays presented provide a range of insights into the empirical reality of labor markets and the complexity of different employment situations. At the same time, they show a concern with theoretical relevance, leading the reader to enter into several of the important debates which have been taking place, often without sufficient reference to one another, around the central question of how sociology can best capture the differentiations of the various groups of working people.

No discussion on the division of labor can ignore the significance of gender as the most important factor in dividing workers. The rapid increase in the size of the female labor force has been one of the most significant features of industrialized countries. The literature on this topic spans many disciplines and draws attention to the ways in which the position of women workers is determined by the sexual division of labor, and by women's role in reproductive, domestic and productive work, as a whole. The entries in this section are about the types of work women do and their position in the changing labor market, about how and why women come to be in jobs typically regarded as semi or unskilled, and about women workers' consciousness as workers and as women. These entries look at the interplay between gender and class, the impact of the new technology on women, and women's position in the new international division of labor. They reveal the complexity of the work women do, and bring out the differences and similarities in women's work experiences cross-culturally.

Chapter three shows that the new technology has already had an impact on our lives, and that there is hardly any need to provide any explanation of why the topic is significant. However, there is a growing concern and debate about the implications of technological change for work. Fears of a major displacement of labor, and also of de-skilling, have aroused considerable discussion and anxiety. Some argue that the dominant effect of the new technology will be to de-skill the work force, destroy the craft occupations, and fragment jobs into meaningless elements which can be performed by unskilled operators, controlled by large-scale bureaucracies run in the interest of international capital. Others suggest that it will be the automated machinery and systems which will take over all the routine tasks. Thus, the impact of the new technology will be to require a more highly educated and trained work force to perform complex tasks which need a high level of the human decision-making skill. Such jobs will therefore give autonomy and variety to the worker. The debate is, in other words, about whether the new technology is likely to lead to proletarianization or professionalization.

Not only is there a dispute about the long-term effects of the new technology on skill levels; there is also, closely bound up with this issue, the question of how jobs of the future will be organized. What might the internal organization of the office and the factory of the future look like? To what extent will the new technology destroy or create jobs? Which groups of workers, which industries, and which types of work will be the most affected? The entries in this section make it clear that the impact of rapid technological change has been uneven. Many workers remained untouched, while others have known technical change in a relatively small way, change which has been absorbed in working practices with little threat of dislocation. Still others have been greatly affected in their particular industry or occupation.

Related to the concern over the impact of technology is the growing debate on unemployment. Unemployment has become the plague of the 1980's, and there is much debate and question over its cause, nature and impact. What is the prospect before us? Is a return to full employment achievable? And, if so, within what time span? Is the ending of mass unemployment merely a matter of economic priorities and political will, or have the prevailing economic realities undergone a fundamental change?

Some analysts think that plant closure and unemployment is a transitory phenomenon that reflects a natural adjustment in the economy and labor force. Others argue that unemployment and dislocated workers are chronic problems that stem from fundamental changes in the operation of the market at a global level. Are the current global, technological and internal economic constraints such that we must concede that a major quantitative increase in the total number of jobs is now unlikely in the mid-term and that a return to our previous patterns of full employment will continue to be frustrated during the foreseeable future? These quantitative issues form one strand of the present debate over unemployment.

The loss of the ideal of full employment poses a serious challenge to the adequacy of the present social and economic system. Moreover, the loss of work involves much more than a consequent loss of income. Work plays a very important role in individuals lives. There are many unanswered questions about what happens to people and their families, their communities, and the social and economic fabric of the society, following the loss of jobs. How severe are the immediate emotional shocks to workers and their families? Is some form of trauma, breakdown, or violent reaction a common response? How do workers affected at different stages in their working lives, with different amounts of skill and education, and in different social situations vary in their responses? How many look for, and find, new jobs? Must they often accept, and are they willing to take, jobs that are less satisfactory in pay, status, location, and/or working conditions?

Another concern related to employment, or the lack of it, is the issue of occupational hazards. The literature on occupational health and safety shows that our work places not only produce commodities, goods, and services, but also affect the attitudes of workers and, more importantly, produce wounds and cause deaths. Job hazards are not limited to heavy industries, but are connected with various types of occupations. Occupational hazards pose threats that extend beyond the work place itself. Workers can expose their families to health risks and the long reach of occupational diseases even extends to future generations.

The entries, in this next section, place work and health in a wider conceptual framework, and reveal the extent, types and variations of work-related injuries and diseases. More importantly, they show that the most significant feature of occupational diseases and injuries is that, in principle, they are preventable. The achievements made in other countries, and by alternative forms of organizations in this area, call the traditional approach to occupational health and safety into question. What is necessary is an entirely fresh focus, with the joint involvement of workers, unions, government and employers. The central key to progress in this area lies in the cultivation of the workers' involvement in it. The employees' own lives and health are at stake in the work place, and truly adequate protection will not develop until the individual workers become aware of all the dangers of the work place, these dangers' dimensions, and alternatives that can furnish reasonable safeguards. The challenge, therefore, is to make occupational health and safety a central part of the workers' everyday life by giving them control over their work place environment.

Unions have been a major means through which workers have tried to influence their work relations. In today's uncertain world, more than ever before, trade unions are facing serious challenges. There are developments on the management side which have far reaching implications for labor organizations in industrialized countries. The internal dynamics of labor union development have been decisively affected by the changes in the labor market, the structure and organization of work, and the social composition of the labor force. Also, the movement of the labor force from manufacturing to the service sector, the restructuring of the world economy, the new international division of labor, the increasing participation of women in the labor market, and the expansion in part-time and flexible forms of work are calling the traditional union structure and strategy into question, and are affecting the balance of power between management and labor.

There has been abundant evidence of women workers' ill-treatment on the part of organized labor. Many unions have a history of excluding women from membership altogether, and virtually all have tended to exclude them from positions of power. Furthermore, unions have often acted to reinforce, rather than challenge sexual inequality in the labor market. As well, governments are increasingly intervening to influence collective bargaining, causing even more difficulties for trade unions.

The entries in this section on unions seek to come to terms with the complex issues that face organized labor today. They take up a wide range of specific subjects. Some are case studies of workers' participation in individual unions, organizing efforts, or strikes; others examine broader themes in labor history, focusing on a specific time period and country; and still others explore the situation of particular categories of workers over a longer time span. The bibliography offers more nuanced perspectives on women's labour history, by examining the structural characteristics of unionism, on the one hand, and the impact of broader social ideology about gender on the labor movement, on the other, shedding new light on this critical problem. Although the entries are written from a variety of perspectives, as a whole, they bring out the complex relationship between gender, class, and ethnicity.

There has always been, of course, interest and experimentation in alternative forms of the organization of work relations, as well as work 'humanization' techniques. And there are now overwhelming arguments for more democracy in the workplace. The democratic case within industry has the same basis as democratic arguments elsewhere--that all individuals should have a say in those decisions which affect their lives. When democratic values are broadly accepted throughout the rest of the society, it is all the more difficult to deny their validity within the shop, factory or office.

Employees, particularly those of a young generation accustomed to their liberal democratic ideas of their western world, are starting to reject an industrial system in which human needs are still given too low a priority. They are demanding not only more satisfying work, but also a greater say in the running of their work enterprises. They are becoming more concerned with the quality of their working life, health and safety, and environmental issues. Employees question management as much as any other authority; so much so that it is becoming increasingly hard to run industry in the traditional way. What is now required is nothing less than a new basis for consent.

The entries in this part, **industrial democracy**, present a number of important changes which have occurred in the patterns of management and structure of decision-making in various countries. They identify the range and main features of participation, and discuss a number of important themes and practices in work place relations and managerial styles, as they are being practiced, rethought, and refashioned. They also look at new trends in working-time arrangement, and challenge the claim that efficient and rational organization can be achieved only through highly bureaucratic organizations. They, furthermore, pose many important questions regarding organizational structures in democratic work places and investigate the possibility for their widespread application.

CHAPTER ONE

THE WORLD OF WORK

Ideology of Work

1. Aho, S. "Labour Society in Crisis? A Discussion."
   Acta Sociologica, 28(1) 1985, 55-61.

   Hannah Ardent used the concept of labor
   society to criticize modern age life and thinking
   for worshiping labor and neglecting all other
   human conditions. Sociologists have increasingly
   been using this concept to refer to industrial
   societies; it is claimed that in modern Western
   societies the economic, moral and social order is
   labor--in a way which is without parallel in
   history.
   Provocative, this discussion shows that the
   labor society is in crisis.

2. Ali, A., M. Al-Shakhis. "Managerial Beliefs about
   Work in two Arab States." **Organization
   Studies**, 10(2) 1989, 169-186.

   Shows that Saudi and Iraqi executives are not
   homogeneous groups. Their country affiliation,
   rather than demographic or organizational
   variables, is found to be more important in
   influencing work orientations. Iraqi managers
   tend to have more egalitarian and humanistic
   beliefs about work than do Saudi managers.
   Of particular value to those interested in
   comparative industrial behavior.

3. Anthony, P.D. **The Ideology of Work.** London:
   Tavistock, 1977.

   Analyses the various ideologies that have
   been developed to persuade people to work.
   Ideologies are necessary because work for most
   people, has always been associated with danger and
   unpleasantness. This preoccupation with ideology
   is highly developed in both advanced capitalist
   and state socialist countries.
   Provides a fascinating account of the ideas
   that have been used to justify work.

4. Beaty, D. T. and O. Harari. "South Africa: White
      Managers, Black Voices." **Harvard Business
      Review**, 65(4) 1987, 98.

      Many of the terms used by Western scholars of
industrial relations can, in South Africa, mean
something quite different to blacks than they do
to the whites. While white managers see the work
place as separate from politics, black workers see
it as an extension of apartheid. Productivity
seems to be inseparable from politics in this
country.
      Excellent evidence of the complex links
between politics, work attitudes and productivity.

   * *Brecher, J. (Item 79)*
   * *Burawoy, M. (Item 39)*

5. Cannings, K. "Managerial Promotion: The Effects of
      Socialization, Specialization and Gender."
      Industrial and Labour Relations Review, 42(1)
      1988, 77-88.

      Reports the results of a survey of managers
in a large Canadian corporation, showing that
women managers earn much less than their male
counterparts and are less likely to be promoted.
      Shows the decisive impact of gender ideology
on work and mobility.

6. Chang, S.K.C. "Managerial Attitudes and Leadership
      Power in U.S. Companies in Taiwan, R.O.C."
      **International Journal of Comparative
      Sociology**, 28(1-2) 1987, 14-29.

      Examines the differences in management style
between top level Chinese and American managers of
U.S. companies in Taiwan, finding that these
managers tend to follow almost identical patterns
of management style. Thus, the policy of
multinational corporations in Taiwan, which limits
the promotion of Chinese managers into upper level
positions, appears to be without empirical
foundation.

Provides a solid basis for developing corporate policies and staffing decisions.

7. Cherrington, D.J. **The Work Ethic: Working Values and Values that Work**. New York: Amacom, 1980.

Increased government regulation, inadequate investment, and a less co-operative attitude between business and government have been cited as some of the factors which have caused a decline in productivity in America. Cherrington believes these factors are important, but do not explain the whole story. The missing factor is referred to as the X factor, which is identified with the changing values of the employees--values that differ substantially from the traditional work ethic.
Of particular interest to those concerned with normative aspects of work productivity.

8. Coles, R. "Storytellers' Ethics." **Harvard Business Review**, 65(2) 1987, 8.

Provides a survey of selected literature, raising important questions on how individuals conduct their lives, as well as the impact of their actions on society.
An illuminating and innovative addition to the study of the business ethic.

* *Doering, M. (Item 141)*

9. Edwards, P.K. <u>Managing the Factory: A Survey of General Managers</u>. Oxford: Blackwell, 1987.

Examines the attitudes of managers and their involvement in the management of labor in large corporations. There is little support for the simplistic 'macho management' type of analysis, in which union-bashing and the fear of unemployment are used to gain compliance. Instead, the managers' focus is on improving their employer's

competitive position through greater flexibility
and enhanced productivity.
    Redirects the focus of analysis from that of
the managed to the managers. Useful to academics
and managers, as well as those who have an
interest in industrial relations.

* *Jackson, R.M. (Item 54)*
* *Jencks, C. (Item 97)*
* *Le Masters, E.E. (Item 102)*
* *Mies, M. (Item 26)*

10. MOW International Research Team. **The Meaning of
    Working**, London: Academic Press, 1987

        Uses national representative samples of the
    work force, and selected socially important target
    groups, to investigate, within industrialized
    nations, the meaning people attach to their work.
    Assesses the meaning of working in Belgium,
    Britain, The Federal Republic of Germany, Israel,
    Japan, the Netherlands, the USA, and Yugoslavia;
    summarizes the main findings, and explores
    possible action and policy implications.
        An important addition to the field of
    occupational and organizational psychology.

    * *Newman, K.S. (Item 104)*

11. Ogunbameru, O.A. "The African Proletariat in
    Industrial Employment: A Reappraisal."
    International Social Science Journal, 36(100)
    1984, 341-354.

        Questions the common portrayal of African
    workers as unproductive, inefficient, uncommitted
    to their work and prone to high turnover,
    demonstrating instead that low productivity and
    lack of commitment are not innate features of
    African workers, but the consequence of factors
    such as constant breakdown of machines, lack of
    security, low and irregular pay and poor working
    conditions.
        A contribution to the literature on work
    attitude.

12. Pahl, R.E. **On Work: Historical, Comparative and Theoretical Approaches**, Oxford: Basil Blackwell, 1988.

Aims to clarify the confusion and ambiguities about work--its meaning, nature and purpose in our lives. Examines the past experiences of work, the emergence of new patterns of work, work done by women--paid and unpaid, domestically, work outside employment--and the new forces of today's capitalist economy--from home working to the new factories in the Third World.

A remarkable collection of studies, this publication provides an in-depth view of various dimensions of work. An excellent textbook for sociology of work.

* *Plath, D.W. (Item 106)*

13. Prandy, K., A. Stewart, and R.M. Blackburn. **White Collar Work**. London: Macmillan Press, Ltd., 1982.

Examines how white collar workers experience work, and how they respond when the rewards of work do not correspond to their experiences. Also looks at the level of rewards individuals receive, the expectations workers hold about their jobs, and assesses how workers try to change their situations.

Has much to offer on workers' attitudes toward their jobs and unions. Raises important methodological questions when measuring expectations.

14. Rezsohazy, R. "Recent Social Development and Changes in Attitudes to Time." **International Social Science Journal**, 38(107) 1986, 33-48.

The way people regard and employ time is largely dependent on their economic conditions, the organization of their daily life and their cultural setting, including religion. Ideas about, and attitudes to, time have a deep impact

on people's economic behavior, political actions,
and their relationships in the various sectors of
society. Identifies the new attitudes with regard
to the passage of time in its past, present and
future dimensions.

Helpful for understanding variations in work
attitudes in different societies.

15. Shlapentokh, V. "Evolution in the Soviet Sociology
    of Work: From Ideology to Pragmatism." **Work
    and Occupations**, 14(3) 1987, 410-433.

Traces the sociology of work in the Soviet
Union through a number of different periods which
are characterized by the dominance of different
theoretical and ideological orientations. The
Soviet sociology of work has changed considerably
since its emergence in the late 1950's. In fact,
in recent years, Soviet sociologists of work have
been able to develop a variety of approaches which
enrich our understanding of workers' attitudes.

* *Triska, J.F. (Item 123)*

16. Wallman, S. **Social Anthropology of Work**, New York:
    Academic Press, 1979.

Uses the Marxist debate, and case studies
from pre-industrial to advanced industrial
societies, to explore the concept of work from
various points of view. It takes a broad, cross-
cultural frame of reference, and places work in
the context of social relationships and symbolic
values. It also describes very well the
experience and organization of work in a variety
of social structures, paying particular attention
to the systematic relation between culture,
organization and structure.

Well-organized and informative. Ideal for a
complementary textbook for a course on the
sociology of work.

* *Westsood, S. (Item 230)*
* *Willis, P. (Item 128)*
* *Wipper, A. (Item 129)*

Understanding the Global Dimension

17. Alden, V.R. "Who Says you Can't Crack Japanese
    Market?" **Harvard Business Review**, 65(1)
    1987, 52.

    Questions myths about the Japanese market:
    That they are not serious about opening their
    market; that they have high trade barriers; and
    that their government helps them to penetrate
    foreign markets. On the contrary, shows that the
    American companies have entered Japan's seemingly
    impenetrable market and are thriving.
    An important contribution for understanding
    the present economic relations at the world level.

18. Beneria, L. and M. Roldan. **The Crossroads of
    Class and Gender: International Homework,
    Subcontracting, and Household Dynamics in
    Mexico City.** Chicago: University of Chicago
    Press, 1987.

    The recent global restructuring and economic
    recession created conditions in both
    industrialized and industrializing countries that
    have encouraged employers and workers to seek
    greater flexibility in their work arrangements.
    Homework provides such flexibility and enables
    workers to cope with high unemployment rates, and
    it also increases the family budget. Homeworkers
    offer firms a mechanism that can lower the costs
    of production and avoid conflict with their
    unions.
    The exploration of the mutual reinforcement
    of class and gender at home and in the capitalist
    economy is among this work's major contributions.

19. Bessant, J., S. Cole. **Stacking the Chips:
    Information Technology and the Distribution
    of Income.** London: Frances Pinter, 1985.

    This book takes the world economy for its
    framework and examines the probable changes in

employment and income for six groups of countries.
Considers the possible consequences of both
systematic and non-systematic technical change,
which involves the reorganization of production
throughout the economy. The primary message is
that the provision of adequate employment to the
working population everywhere, and improving the
distribution of income, cannot be left to the
blind forces of technological change, assisted by
piecemeal measures of intervention by any
particular group.
    Brings out the complexity of the
interdependence between developed and developing
countries and helps to understand the effects of
the new technology on employment and income.

* *Bluestone, B. (Item 269)*
* *Cornfield, D.B. (Item 335)*

20. Dickson, D.N. "Self-help from Japan." **Harvard
    Business Review,** 64(1) 1986, 8.

    The message of this discussion is that the
Japanese have changed the course of international
corporate competition. Unless international
executives study the forces behind the Japanese
success, they may not understand what they will
have to do to succeed in the world market.
    Introduces important sets of books which can
help to better understand today's competitive
world market and its impact on industrial
relations

* *De Vos, D. (Item 237)*
* *Euzeby, A. (Item 385)*

21. Ferleger, L. and J.R. Mandle. "Democracy and
    Productivity in the Future of American
    Economy." **Review of Radical Political
    Economy.** 19(4) 1987, 1-15.

    Offers a strategy to restore the United
States' economic competitiveness, involving the
control of international capital mobility, a
reduction in the military budget, a stimulating

fiscal and monetary policy, and an income policy.
Suggests that the adoption of such a strategy will
bring full employment, growth in productivity,
democratization and egalitarianism.

An important study for understanding the
debate on the contemporary crisis in the American
economy

22. Fröbel, F., J. Heinrichs and O. Kreye. **The New
    International Division of Labour: Structural
    Unemployment in Industrialized Countries and
    Industrialization in Developing Countries.**
    Cambridge: Cambridge University Press, 1980.

Shows that a major shift has occurred in the
international division of labor, which involved
the transfer of a large section of industrial
production to cheap labor countries of the Third
World, Southern Europe and even Eastern Europe.
Rising unemployment in industrialized capitalist
countries is seen as a reflection of increasing
worldwide competition between workers for jobs and
of the emergence of a world market in production
sites.

A most welcome addition, which provides a
comprehensive survey of the growth of free zones
in developing countries and the
internationalization of capital.

23. Grunwald, J. and K. Flamm, **The Global Factory:
    Foreign Assembly in International Trade.**
    Washington, D.C.: The Brookings Institution,
    1985.

Examines industrial collaboration between
developed and developing countries, and answers
broad sets of questions in interpreting the recent
trends in the internationalization of industry:
how important are overseas production
arrangements? What are their characteristics?
What are the causes of growth in overseas
production?, and how does it affect the home and
host economies?

An important addition for understanding the
environment within which today's employer and
employees have to operate.

* Jacobi, O. (Item 344)

24. Kaplinsky, R. **Automation: The Technology and
     Society.** London: Longman, 1984.

     Discusses the historical link between the
diffusion of automation technologies and the
progress of economies. The economic recession and
depression of the late 1970's and early 1980's
have sharply raised the competitive pressures in
the economy. Automation has been adopted in
response to the economic crisis. Assesses the
impact of the new automation technologies upon
society.
     As an analysis of contemporary trends in the
automation in the manufacturing firms, this book
makes an excellent and original contribution.

(A rejoinder to 253)

25. Kolko, J. **Restructuring the World Economy.** New
     York: Pantheon Books, 1988.

     Provides a powerful and rich account of the
current crisis in global capitalism. Explores
what this crisis means for the United States,
Japan and Western Europe; for less developed
nations; and for the centrally planned economies
of Eastern Europe, Russia and China. Explores
chronologically the interaction of major factors
since the beginning of the crisis in 1974 and
analyzes the relation between the crisis and the
system--capital labor and the state.
     A must reading for grasping the contemporary
nature of the restructuring of the economy and its
implication for employment.

26. Mies, M. **The Lace Makers of Narsapur: Indian
     Housewives Produce for the World Market.**
     London: Zed Press for ILO, 1982.

        Provides a dramatic case of labor market
segmentation by caste and by gender. The women
lace makers are exploited by the traders and
owners of the industry, and receive only a portion
of the wage of female agricultural laborers in the
same district. These women come from a high, but
impoverished caste whose strong notion of what
is appropriate for women prevents them from taking
on any work which would remove their secluded
status as housewives.
        An excellent study. Brings out the interplay
between caste, class and gender.

27. Morehouse, W. **American Labour in a Changing World
       Economy**, New York: Praeger, Publisher, 1978.

        Discusses employment in a rapidly changing
economy, exploring the impact of organizations,
trade and foreign investments on jobs in the
United States and other countries. It examines
the problems associated with establishing
meaningful collective bargaining with
multinational corporations. Also discussed are
the role of labor in the Third World development
and the meaning of a new direction in the
international and political system for American
workers. Makes it clear that although times have
changed, international economic policies affecting
employment have not.
        An important piece for understanding
contemporary economic restructuring at the
international level.

28. Olson, G.M. (ed.). **Industrial Change and Labour
       Adjustment in Sweden and Canada.** Toronto:
       Garmond Press, 1988.

        Addresses the rapid changes that the
industrialized world is facing; changes that mean
harsher global competition and accelerated
technological change in products and processes.
Reviews how Canada and Sweden managed the process
of rapid change and labor adjustment both
efficiently and equitably.

     Brings together ideas from a large number of
labor experts: government, academics, private
sector, labor unions and activists.

29. Payne, G.   "Deindustrialization and Occupational
         Mobility." **The British Journal of Sociology**,
         38(2) 1987, 255-265.

     Provides new evidence on mobility in five
industrial sectors, and illustrates the
relationship between growth of each sector, growth
of non-manual occupations, and the opportunity for
mobility. Mobility patterns did not change in the
1970's and early 1980's, but the trend has been
towards a modified picture of inequality in favor
of non-manual workers.
     Useful insights on the stratification of the
labor force in the industrialized societies are
provided in this entry.

30. Perlmutter, H.V. and D. A. Heenan, "Cooperate to
         Compete Globally." **Harvard Business Review**,
         64(2) 1986, 136.

     Discusses the growing global competition and
the trend towards a higher concentration of
capital. It reviews global partnership as the
most profitable route to future opportunities.
Few companies and few nations will prosper in the
world economy without some sort of global
strategic partnership. Also shows the growing
centralization of the world economy, along with
joint ventures by the tricentres of economic
power: the United States, Western Europe and
Japan.
     A must reading for understanding the context
within which labor and capital operate.

31. Piore, M.J. and C.F. Sabel. **The Second Industrial
         Divide: Possibilities for Prosperity.** New
         York: Basic Books Inc., 1984.

Claims that the technologies and operating procedures of most modern corporations--the forms of labor market control defended by many labor movements, the instrument of macroeconomic control developed by bureaucrats and economists in the welfare states, and the rules of the international monetary and trading systems established after World War II--must all be modified, perhaps even discarded, if the chronic economic diseases of our time are to be cured.

An excellent study which has generated a lot of debate. Addresses important issues necessary for understanding work and industry in industrialized countries.

(A rejoinder to Item 25)

32. Reich, R. B. and E. D. Mankin. "Joint Ventures with Japan Give Away our Future." **Harvard Business Review,** 64(2) 1986, 78.

Comments on aspects of a trend that is reshaping America's trade relations with Japan and creating a new context for international competition. Japanese companies are setting up plants in the United States, either as joint ventures or on their own. This is part of the Japanese strategy to increase its competitive edge.

Shows the new dimensions of the international economy, as well as the problems facing workers and managers in the United States.

(A rejoinder to Item 17)

33. Schwarz, J.E. and T.J. Volgy. "The Myth of America's Economic Decline." **Harvard Business Review,** 63(5) 1985, 98.

Questions the common belief that the American economy suffered a long cycle of economic decline from 1965 to 1980. On the contrary, the presumed period is seen as a time of unrecognized success. Believes that the government policies misdiagnosed the disease and therefore brought

negative side effects--a budget deficit, trade
imbalance and widespread social inequality.
Provides a provocative outlook of the recent
debate on the crisis of the American economy.

(Rebutted by Item 20)

34. Sinclair, S. **The World Car: The Future of the
Automobile Industry.** New York: Facts on File
Publications, 1983.

Asks whether the concept of the 'world car',
a strategy developed in the 1980's will remain as
important as was initially expected. Analyses the
current state of the car market, and discusses the
major issues which will affect its future.
An important case study which highlights some
of the factors affecting the world industrial
structure as a whole in the 1980's.

35. Spector, N.   "Managing for Competitiveness."
Canadian Public Administration, 30(2) 1987,
230-242.

Compares the ways in which the private and
public sectors of the economy of industrialized
countries responded to the worldwide recession of
1981-1982. While the private and public sectors
faced different impediments, management used
similar strategies to overcome them. The aim was
to promote competitiveness, in order to be able to
meet the challenges of the new international
economic environment.
Brings out some of the issues that managers
have to face in today's competitive economy.

Work Relations and Work Organizations:
A Historical Perspective

36. Attewell, P. "The De-skilling Controversy." **Work and Occupations**, 14(3) 1987, 323-346.

    Draws upon a wide range of literature, and presents theoretical, empirical and methodological criticisms of the de-skilling thesis. Suggests that the profit motive does not necessarily drive managers to de-skill their labor force and, moreover, that unskilled jobs constitute only a part of the work force. Concludes that de-skilling has not been a dominant trend of occupational change.
    Essential for understanding the debate on de-skilling.

    (Rebutted by Item 38)

37. Bean, R. **Comparative Industrial Relations: An Introduction to Cross-National Perspective,** London: Croom Helm, 1985.

    Presents an introduction to the domain of industrial relations through a survey and an integration of recent literature from various perspectives on the topic. It focuses on central themes and topics, rather than individual countries. Also covers each of the major themes in industrial relations and incorporates materials from North America, Western Europe, Japan, Australia, and some centrally planned and underdeveloped countries.
    The first introductory text on this important topic.

38. Braverman, H. **Labor and Monopoly Capital: The Degradation of Work in the Twentieth Century.** New York: Monthly Review Press, 1974.

    Combines Marx's class analysis with the studies of labor process and stratification, and

shows that the development of capitalism resulted
in the workers' progressive loss of skill and
control over the labor process. The application
of Taylor's scientific management speeded this
process and had a major effect on the nature of
work, the structure of occupations, and the
movement of people from one job to another. It
lowered the craft skill and degraded the work.
    Braverman's thesis has been most widely
debated and is a must for understanding many of
the discussions on the labor process.

(Rebutted by Item 243)

39. Burawoy, M. **The Politics of Production: Factory**
        Regimes under Capitalism and Socialism.
        London: New Left Books, 1985.

        Analyses shop-floor institutions and their
characteristic patterns of power and conflict, and
attempts to determine the mechanisms that generate
consent on the shop floor. Claims that workers
reproduce the economic conditions for the
maintenance of their exploitation and at the same
time reproduce political and ideological relations
that mask the reality of their exploitation.
Provides detailed illustration from case studies
of industrial establishments in the United States,
United Kingdom, Hungary and Zambia between 1950-
1970.
        The best account of how rational-legal
domination is legitimized in work places.

40. Chandler, A.D. **The Visible Hand: The Managerial**
        Revolution in American Business, Cambridge:
        The Belknap Press of Harvard University
        Press, 1977.

        Examines the changing process of production
and distribution in the United States, and the
ways in which it has been managed. Shows that the
modern business enterprise took the place of
market mechanisms in co-ordinating the activities
of the economy. The visible hand of management
was replaced by what Adam Smith called the

invisible hand of market forces. Also
demonstrates the extent to which managers have
exerted influence in determining the size and
concentration of American industry.
   An excellent scholarship, of particular
interest to students of business and management.

41. Clawson, D. **Bureaucracy and the Labor Process:
       The Transformation of U.S. Industry, 1860–
       1920.** New York: Monthly Review Press, 1980.

   Reviews the process by which American
industry was transformed from a nonbureaucratic to
predominantly bureaucratic form of organization.
Questions the conception of bureaucracy as highly
rational, efficient and class neutral. Presents a
picture of inside contracting as capable of high
quality mass production within a hierarchical, but
nonbureaucratic structure. Provides a careful
synthesis of empirical and theoretical materials.
   A significant contribution for understanding
the historical transformation of the work place
under capitalism.

(A rejoinder to Item 38)

42. Cockburn, C. **Brothers: Male Dominance and
       Technological Change.** London: Pluto Press,
       1983.

   Technological change has affected the task of
compositors, their labor market position and their
work environment, and this work looks at the
compositor's reaction to this process of change.
Shows how employers, unions, and technology mold
workers' beliefs and indicates how composing
almost became a female occupation in the 19th
century, before male workers asserted their
control.
   Brings out the ambiguities of the concept of
skill, and the limitations of simple 'de-skilling'
theories of technological change.

(A rejoinder to Items 38, 41)

43. Crompton, R. and G. Jones. **White Collar
    Proletariat: De-skilling and Gender in
    Clerical Work.** London: Macmillan, 1984.

     Focuses on the themes of de-skilling and the
class location of white-collar employees to reveal
the importance of gender in the career structure
of clerical workers. Makes the important point
that white-collar workers cannot be treated as a
homogeneous group, and shows that 'professional
qualities' discriminate against women. However,
the stability of male-based career structures is
threatened by the change in attitude and character
of women in clerical work.
     A valuable addition to the debate on de-
skilling and to our understanding of the
importance of gender for defining class.

44. Edwards, P.K. **Conflict at Work, A Materialist
    Analysis of Work-place Relations.** Oxford:
    Basil Blackwell, 1986.

     Shows that relations at the point of
production have a 'relative autonomy' from the
influences of outside economic and social forces,
and that this relative autonomy is based on
'customs and traditions' inherent in the labor
process itself. The external factors are always
transformed into, and thereby often heavily
modified by the specific configuration and
traditions of the single work process.
     A stimulating contribution to the literature
on the labor process. Helps to clarify many of the
obscure distinctions in the ongoing debate.

     * *Edwards, P. K. (Item 9)*

45. Esland, G. and G. Salaman (eds.). **The Politics of
    Work and Occupations.** London: Open
    University Press, 1980.

     Brings together the theoretical perspectives
which surround the sociology of work, successfully
examines the important areas in industrial

sociology and shows the extent to which the post-Braverman debate has enriched the field. Assembles a number of authoritative essays, ranging from the nature of work in Nazi Germany concentration camps to a critique of management ideology.

An excellent reader for students of industrial sociology. Offers access to a wide ranging body of literature in the field.

46. Friedland, W. H., A.E. Barton and R.J. Thomas. **Manufacturing Green Gold: Capital, Labour, Technology in the Lettuce Industry.** Cambridge: Cambridge University Press, 1981.

Analyses the labor process in the lettuce industry as part of a broader comparative analysis of productive systems and never loses sight of the theoretical concerns. Charts the historical growth of lettuce production, vertical integration and concentration in the industry, the role of the state in this process and the impact of all these factors on the organization of the labor process.

A remarkable study which successfully combines theoretical discussion with the empirical findings.

47. Garon, S. **The State and Labour in Modern Japan.** Berkeley: University of California Press, 1988.

Provides an account of state corporatism in Japan during the war. Discusses the limits of employers' reliance on the tradition of paternalism to maintain harmonious labor relations. During the wartime atmosphere of the 1930s, Japanese bureaucrats imposed stringent control over both capital and labor in order to minimize labor management conflict. Unions also willingly accepted the state's intervention in regulating employees.

Of value not only to students of Japanese labour history, but also to those interested in comparative labor history.

(A rejoinder to Items 66, 105)

48. Goodman, P.S., R.S. Atkin et al. **Absenteeism: New Approaches to Understanding, Measuring, and Managing Employee Absence**. San Francisco: Jossey-Bass, 1984.

    Reviews research on the definition and measurement of absenteeism and provides a useful taxonomy of questions for evaluating published studies. Brings conceptual clarity to the complex relationships between absenteeism upon various forms of worker withdrawal. Describes the impact of absenteeism in individuals and organizations. Focuses on policy issues, and reviews different means of increasing employee attendance. Notable for its overall quality and its attempt to integrate the vast body of theoretical and empirical work on absenteeism.

49. Gordon, D., R.Edwards, and M. Reich. **Segmented Work, Divided Workers: The Historical Transformation of Labor in the United States**. Cambridge: Cambridge University Press, 1982.

    Rejects the popular approach, which divides the United States economic development into competitive and monopoly capitalism. Instead proposes that the system has passed through three stages, with each stage representing a unique solution to the problem of capital accumulation. A social structure of accumulation is created in the consolidation phase of each stage.
    Successfully combines a detailed historical description with a theoretical framework. Sheds light on the problem of the capitalist-worker relationship.

50. Gospel, H.F., and C.R. Littler (eds.). **Managerial Strategies and Industrial Relations**. London: Heinemann Educational Books, 1983.

    Deals with the critical role that management plays in the development of industrial relations.

Through case studies from several countries--
Britain, Germany, the United States and Japan--
this work explains the variations in control
patterns. The overall message is that management
reacted to changing market conditions by relying
more on indirect forms of control, as opposed to
direct forms of control.

A rich addition to industrial relations
literature, especially useful for its comparative
dimension and theoretical contribution.

51. Hill, S. **Competition and Control at Work: The New
Industrial Sociology.** Cambridge: The MIT
Press, 1981.

Suggests that profitability within
conventional capitalist and socialist economies
appears to depend on depriving employees of their
independence and ensuring their subordination.
Shows persuasively that there is a tension between
co-operation and competition in the economic
activity. Makes the point that industrial
relations entail relations between classes, and
that regulation of industrial conflict ought to be
seen as the institutionalization of class
conflict.

A sophisticated textbook, rich in theory,
which presents the reader with a useful update on
research coming out of Britain and attempts to
reconstruct the field of industrial sociology.

(A rejoinder to Item 156)

52. Humphrey, J. **Capitalist Control and Workers'
Struggle in the Brazilian Auto Industry.**
Princeton: Princeton University Press, 1982.

Provides a background of the recent history
of Brazil, particularly the impact of the
Brazilian 'miracle' on the working class. Both
union and management have developed conscious
strategies to deal with a changing economic
situation, however, in the case of Brazil, the
development of industrial capitalism has generated

a working class in the auto industry similar to
that of an industrial country.
    An excellent piece of careful research, with
important theoretical implications. Provides
considerable data on wages, working conditions and
workers' attitudes.

53. International Labour Organization. **New Forms of**
    Work Organization. 2 vols. Geneva:
    International Labour Organization, 1979.

    Discusses new forms of work organization, and
is a part of a series of activities launched by
the ILO with regard to improvements in the
organization of work. The first volume looks at
Denmark, Norway and Sweden, France, the Federal
Republic of Germany, the United Kingdom and the
United States. The second volume deals with the
German Democratic Republic, India, Italy, the
USSR, and is complemented by a section on the
economic costs and benefits of new forms of work
organization.
    There is much to be learned from the national
monographs presented here.

54. Jackson, R.M. **The Formation of Craft Labor**
    Markets. New York: Academic Press, 1984.

    Explains how internal labor markets in
carpentry and printing developed in the United
States by the unions obtaining significant input
into decisions concerning hiring, job assignments
and work procedures. Here, there were
technological and economic impediments which
prevented employers from dispensing with skilled
labor. Ideological and organizational factors
were as important as economic factors in shaping
the craft labor market.
    An essential reading for its critical stand
on the main debates in industrial sociology.

55. Kalleberg, A.L. and I. Berg. **Work and Industry:**
    Structures, Markets, and Processes. New
    York: Plenum Press, 1987.

Aims to integrate recent research done in the United States on the sociology of work and develops a matrix of six work 'structures' and six types of markets that influence the nature of work. The six work structures include the state, classes, occupations, industries, business organizations, and unions. The six types of markets include product markets, capital markets, resource markets, demand for labor, labor supply, and political markets. Criticizes the literature on the sociology of work for not having taken these factors into account.

The coverage is extremely wide; contains a number of pedagogical devices, such as lead questions, which make it useful for a graduate course textbook.

56. Kealey, G.S. **Toronto Workers Respond to Industrial Capitalism, 1867-1892.** Toronto: University of Toronto Press, 1980.

Analyses the making of Toronto's working class and the response of that class to the industrialization process. Discusses formalized working class politics in Toronto: election and voting patterns, the emergence of labor candidates, etc. Shows that workers did not merely respond to the process, but they also shaped what happened.

A substantial contribution to the study of Canadian labor history. Offers a wealth of information.

57. Knights, D., H. Willmott and D. Collinson (eds.). **Job Redesign.** Aldershot: Gower, 1985.

Reflects the new wave of interest that seeks to understand and analyse the social, political and economic conditions and consequences of job design. Many factors such as new technology, changes in labor markets, and the restructuring of corporations as a result of international developments are seen to be crucial. Includes a useful summary of Taylorism, Fordism and Job design.

Offers a coherent line of argument and is an excellent piece for a course on the sociology of work.

58. Kruijt, D. and M. Vellinga. **Labor Relations and Multinational Corporations: The Cerro de Pasco Corporation in Peru (1902-1974)**. Assen:Van Gorcum, 1979 (Distributed in the U.S. by Humanities Press, 1979).

Examines the recent pattern of industrial relations in the mining industry of Peru. Formulates a theory of the development of class consciousness and class conflict. Provides an outline of the history of copper mining in Peru, discussing the economic linkages within the industry and the historical formation of a mining proletariat.
A welcome addition to the sparse English literature on industrial relations in Latin America.

59. Lane, D. **Soviet Labour and the Ethic of Communism: Full Employment and the Labour Process in the USSR**. Boulder, Colorado: Westview Press, 1987.

Attempts to discover the extent to which regular paid labor and a permanent occupation for all who are able to work exist in the Soviet Union. Also looks at whether there are any systematic features of Soviet society, differing from capitalism, which lead to the provision of full employment. Shows that the Soviet economy is one of full employment and labor shortage, and that this affects the labor process by strengthening the position of labor vis-a-vis management; i.e. it leads to low productivity. Thus, a dilemma facing the Soviet economic and political leadership is whether it can increase efficiency and labor productivity within the confine of full employment .
A rich account of the analysis of the labor process in the Soviet Union.

60. Littler, C.R. **The Development of the Labour
    Process in Capitalist Societies; A
    Comprehensive Study of the Transformation of
    Work Organization in Britain, Japan and the
    United States.** London: Heinemann Educational
    Books, Ltd., 1982.

    Provides a theoretical framework for an
    empirical and comparative analysis of forms of
    work organization. Describes the nature and
    timing of Taylorite and non-Taylorite forms of
    work organizations and shows that loss of skill
    neither necessarily began from a craft base, nor
    occurred in a confrontational manner.
    A must for those engaged in the debate on de-
    skilling/up-skilling and the labor process.

    (A rejoinder to Items 38,42)

61. Loveman, G.W. and C. Tilly, "Good Jobs or Bad
    Jobs? Evaluating the American Job Creation
    Experience." **International Labour Review,**
    127(5) 1988, 593-612.

    Demonstrates that jobs with low annual
    earnings have increased among full-time and year-
    round workers, and that earning inequality has
    widened within and between industries and
    occupations. The United States has created a lot
    of poorly paid jobs. In contrast, the European
    countries have been able to keep wages high, but
    have created fewer new jobs. The problem is to
    develop policies that enhance job qualities.
    Describes well the links between slow growth
    and job creation.

62. Marglin, S.A. "What Do Bosses Do? The Origins and
    Functions of Hierarchy in Capitalist
    Production." **Review of Radical Political
    Economy,** 6(2) 1974, 60-112.

    Poses the questions of why, in the course of
    the development of capitalism, workers lost
    control over the production process, what factors

contributed to the formation of the boss-worker
pyramid which characterizes the capitalist mode of
production, and what social function such a
hierarchy serves.
    An illuminating discussion of the development
of a division of labor in industry.

63. Meyer, S. **The Five Dollar Day: Labor Management
        and Social Control In the Ford Motor Company,
        1908-1921.** Albany: State University of New
        York Press, 1981.

    The transformation of work in this case study
involved breaking craft control and using an
abundant supply of cheap immigrant labor. Ford
sought to control workers through the introduction
of a job hierarchy and remodelling the working
class culture. However, the success was
superficial.
    A fine social history and an important
contribution to the study of the labor process.

(A rejoinder to Item 41)

64. Myles, J. "The Expanding Middle: Some Canadian
        Evidence on the Deskilling Debate." **Canadian
        Review of Sociology and Anthropology**, 23(3)
        1988, 335-364.

    Looks at the actual patterns and trends in
the skill distribution of jobs. Demonstrates that
with the growth of a new middle class during the
1960s and '70s, the skill content of the labor
force grew at an accelerated rate. While the
threat of a 'hamburger economy' is real, its
effects have been outweighed by expansion in the
higher skill industries.
    Challenges the simplistic linear thesis on
de-skilling, and illuminates the cleavages within
the working class.

(Rebutted by Item 38)

65. Nelson, D. **Frederick W. Taylor and the Rise of Scientific Management.** Madison: University of Wisconsin Press, 1980.

Attempts to revise the commonly held image of Taylor, known as the father of scientific management. Recognizes Taylor's 'reactionary view' towards workers, but argues that they occupied a small place in Taylor's total system. Suggests that the most persistent resistance to Taylor's system came more from top management than workers.

Provides a complex and intriguing picture of Taylor. A must for those interested on the issue of the development of modern management.

(A rejoinder to Items 38,41)

66. Okochi, K., B. Karsh, and S.B. Levine (eds.). **Workers and Employers in Japan: The Japanese Employment Relations System.** Princeton: Princeton University Press, 1974.

Reviews Japan's industrial relations system, its nature and the prospects for change. Provides a historical background of Japan's industrialization and an overview of changes after World War II. Discusses important issues such as: the transition in the legal framework of the labor system; managers, workers and their organizations; the weakness of the unions; labor disputes and collective bargaining; the reward system and personnel administration; and social security.

An informative and comprehensive addition to the literature on Japan, which can serve as a valuable reference.

(A rejoinder to Items 47, 105, 342)

67. Pagano, U. **Work and Welfare in Economic Theory,** Oxford: Basil Blackwell, 1985.

Criticizes economic theory for treating human labor as a resource, the use of which affects people's welfare only indirectly, and not being able to see the relationship between work and welfare. Beginning with Adam Smith, also evaluates the views of various economists on this issue. Investigates the possibility of developing an institutional arrangement that is capable of economizing on the cost of the organization of production, and which at the same time, considers the welfare and preference of the workers.

An excellent study, and a must for students of labor economics and industrial sociology.

* Pahl, R.E. (Item 12)

68. Rinehart, J. assisted by S. Faber. **The Tyranny of Work: Alienation and the Labour Process**. 2nd edition, Don Mills, Ontario: Harcourt Brace Jovanovich Canada, Inc., 1987.

Follows the thesis of the first edition and discusses the process by which workers have become separated from their means of production. Discusses producers' resistance to the subordination of labor. Challenges the thesis that we have entered a postindustrial society, and criticizes the ideology that workers have been accommodated to the status quo. Treats work under capitalism as an objective social problem which has adverse effects on workers.

A provocative and stimulating contribution to the literature on work.

(A rejoinder to Items 38, 41)

69. Roukis, G. and P.J. Montana. **Work-force Management in the Arabian Peninsula: Forces Affecting Development**. Westport: Greenwood Press, 1986.

Provides the reader with an understanding of the political forces underlying the conflict in the Persian Gulf. It also identifies pivotal factors that influence that area's economic

development, shows how Islam affects and changes
the world of work there, stresses the importance
of understanding the subtleties of cultural
differences and the transfer of technology, and
details manpower problems and labor force
participation in the peninsula.

Gives a solid review of literature on Arab
manpower development in the Gulf, and documents
the dramatic changes in this area since the 1980s.
The recommendations are pertinent to the policy
process.

70. Sabel, C.F. **Work and Politics: The Division of
     Labour in Industry.** Cambridge: Cambridge
     University Press, 1982.

Focuses mainly on France, Great Britain,
Italy, the United States, and West Germany. Finds
that workers' response to employers' moves is
varied. The diversity of their response appears
to vary according to cultural backgrounds,
national history, religious affiliation, and
political and ideological circumstances that
surround work organization. Explores the social
milieu that creates the low-esteem industrial
worker and discusses the transformation of
industrial workers' skills in contemporary
industrial societies.

The wideness of the scope, and the richness
of materials presented here are of great
importance for comparative industrial sociology.

71.   Salaman, G. **Working.** London: Ellis Harwood and
        Tavistock Publications, 1986.

Redirects the sociology of work away from
labor process theory towards the more traditional
concerns of the field. Shows how factors such as
class, gender, and group cultures provide a rich
source for explaining social action in the work
context. Attempts to outline the agenda for a
new sociology of work, by integrating the
theoretical framework with the notion of gender
and class.

A refreshing addition, and valuable for its
theoretical discussion.

72. Stone, K.   "The Origin of Job Structures in the
        Steel Industry." **Radical America**, 7(6) 1973,
        19-64.

        Attempts to examine the development of labor
    market structures in the steel industry. Suggests
    that the institutions of the labor market were not
    the inevitable result of modern technology or a
    complex organization. Instead, they were the
    product of the process through which capitalists
    took over production.
        An important contribution to the debate on
    technology and the process of de-skilling in the
    labor process.

    (A rejoinder to Items 38, 60)

73. Thomas, R.J. **Citizenship, Gender and Work: Social
        Organization of Industrial Agriculture.**
        Berkeley: University of California Press,
        1985.

        Shows how the disadvantaged status of Mexican
    employees is not so much a product of ethnic,
    national or biological differences, but of the
    division of labor in production, the political
    intervention of employers and the system of
    stratification external to the work place.
    Documents how the communal organization of work
    into gangs is linked to the perpetuation of a
    labor system built around workers denied
    citizenship status and rights.
        An impressive study, and an example of how
    citizenship, gender and class integrate.

74. Thompson, P. **The Nature of Work: An Introduction
        to Debates on the Labour Process.** London:
        Macmillan, 1983.

Offers an overview of the argument concerning the increasing degradation of work within capitalism. Captures and criticizes the major issues raised in the debate on the labor process, and imaginatively discusses both the issues of consent and the sexual division of labor. Provides an excellent evaluation of current themes in industrial sociology.

Can be used as a textbook for courses on industrial sociology, the sociology of work and the labor process.

(A rejoinder to Items 38, 42, 60)

* *Wallman, S. (Item 16)*

75. Wood, S. "The Deskilling Debate, New Technology and Work Organization." **Acta Sociologica**, 30(1) 1987, 3-24.

Focuses on the question of alternatives to Taylorism. Questions the unidimensional notion of skill and points to the need for a broader conception of skill, which includes consideration of the 'social construction of skill,' tacit knowledge, and the sexual division of labor. The discussion is linked to the impact of new technology, the effects of recession on work organization, and Japanese management.

A must for those involved in the debate on the labor process.

(Rebutted by Item 38)

76. Wood, S. (ed.). **The Degradation of Work? Skill, Deskilling and the Labour Process.** London: Hutchinson, 1982.

Criticizes Harry Braverman's thesis on deskilling for: employing a weak conception of skill and oversimplifying the impact of industrial capitalism on the transformation of work; overestimating Taylorism and misunderstanding several of its principles; drawing a deterministic link between technological developments and deskilling; and ignoring the complexity of the transition from the craft shop to the modern factory system.

A welcome addition to the post-Braverman debate and a good textbook for a course on the sociology of work.

(Rebutted by Item 38)

Experience of Work and the Structure of the Labor Force

77. Abbot, A. "The New Occupational Structure: What
    Are the Questions?." **Work and Occupations,**
    16(3) 1989, 273-291.

    Shows that the changes in the structure of
the economy over the last half century have given
rise to new questions about occupations and the
division of labor. Provides a critique of the
literature, and makes some predictions about the
future of occupations: service sector jobs--
especially commercial jobs like retail sales will
increase, there will be a deeper division of labor
in most professions, artificial intelligence will
affect many occupations, and computerized worker
surveillance will increase.
    An important addition for understanding the
emerging nature of stratification in
industrialized countries.

78. Blishen, E,R., W.K. Carroll and C. Moore. "The
    1981 Socio-economic Index for Occupations in
    Canada." **The Canadian Review of Sociology and
    Anthropology,** 24(4) 1987, 465-488.

    Provides a socioeconomic index for the
Canadian labor force based on a combination of
income, education and the prestige score for
occupations. Emphasizes that this type of
measurement is abstracted from the class
relations, but is a useful indicator of
inequalities that exist in the technical division
of labor.
    A very useful index for situations where
access to data is limited to occupational titles.

(A rejoinder to Item 103)

79. Brecher, J. and T. Costello. **Common Sense: For
    Hard Times.** Montreal: Black Rose Books, 1979.

The authors write in plain language about the
work people do, what makes it unfair and
unpleasant, and how it could be changed and become
more creative. The basic proposition is that
society is based on the co-operative labor of the
majority of people, but is controlled by the
bureaucrats, politicians, businessmen and
corporate managers. This book points out that
people have great potential and could use this
power to change their daily lives.
An important source for workers' education,
and makes sense out of what goes on around the
worker's everyday life, both on and off the job.

80. Buttari, J.J. (ed.). **Employment and Labour Force
in Latin America**. Vols. I & II. Washington,
D.C.: Organization of American States for
ECIEL, 1979.

Discusses the employment situation in Central
America, Peru, Argentina, Brazil, Costa Rica and
Chile. Looks at unemployment from a variety of
perspectives. The conclusion is 'optimistic' and
stresses the employment creating potential of high
technology industries. However, this optimism is
not justified by the case studies.
Although limited to wage earning and self-
employment, provides valuable information on labor
supply and demand in selected countries.

81. Cole, R.E. **Work, Mobility and Participation: A
Comparative Study of American and Japanese
Industry**. Berkeley: University of California
Press, 1979.

A comparative study of American and Japanese
industry focusing on the nature of the
contemporary employment structure, the emergence
of a permanent employment practice, job mobility,
the relationship between employees and employers
in the decision making process, work design and
redesign movement, and work ethic. Also discusses
the possibilities of adopting the Japanese style
of management.

A significant contribution to comparative
industrial sociology and of great importance for
understanding Japanese organizational behavior.

* *Coles, R. (Item 8)*

82. Dore, R. **British Factory and Japanese Factory:
    The Origins of National Diversity in
    Industrial Relations.** Berkeley: University
    of California Press, 1973.

    Makes a point by point comparison of two
    factories in Japan with two British ones making
    similar products. Provides a systematic detailed
    illustration of the attitudes which underlie what
    Dore calls the 'market-oriented' system in
    Britain and the 'organizational-oriented' system
    in Japan. Concludes that the Japanese system can
    be adopted by industrialized late developers, as
    well as old industrialized countries.
    Uses a wealth of historical evidence,
    provides important insights for policy and appeals
    to those interested in the 'Japanese miracle'.

83. Faradzhev, F.A. "Solving Employment Problems in a
    Labour Surplus Region of the USSR: The Case
    of Azerbaijan." **International Labour Review,**
    126(3) 1987, 337-350.

    While the USSR as a whole is faced with a
    labor shortage, the Republic of Azerbaijan has a
    surplus of manpower. Discusses Azerbaijan's
    efforts to face this problem by developing labor
    intensive industries which could be used as a
    guideline for similar cases in other places.
    Of particular use for manpower planning and
    policy makers.

84. Foote Whyte, W. "From Human Relations to
    Organizational Behaviour: Reflections on the
    Changing Scene." **Industrial and Labour
    Relations,** 40(4) 1987, 487-500.

Reviews the last fifty years of research in
behavioral science. Shows that labor and
management practitioners of today are more
interested in behavioral research than they were
in the 1940s and 1950s and sees an urgent need for
social scientists to go into the field and
document new lines of development to help
practitioners understand trends and possibilities.

Provides an up-to-date introduction to the
field. Of particular interest to managers and
students of industrial behavior.

85. Ford, R.L. **Work, Organization, and Power:
    Introduction to Industrial Sociology**. Boston:
    Allyn and Bacon, Inc., 1988.

Examines a complex set of issues: how
societies change their industrial structures over
time; types of economic organization; the changing
nature of occupational structure; the
concentration of economic and political power
outside and inside the United States; a history of
the labor movement and the problems it faces;
ways in which workers' health is affected by the
influence of power; and what can be done to
alleviate the problems posed by the concentration
of economic and political power.

Pulls together a number of areas in
industrial sociology, and helps to understand the
issues facing us in contemporary society.

86. Frenkel, S.J. "Industrial Sociology and Work-place
    Relations in Advanced Capitalist Societies."
    **International Journal of Comparative
    Sociology**, 27(1-2) 1986, 69-86.

Shows that work place relations are not
determined by either technological or managerial
imperatives, but are the product of a complex
process of interaction between class interests
represented by such organizations as corporations,
unions, state and political parties. Thus, an
explanation of variations in work place relations
in various countries requires sensitivity to

empirical details specific to the case under
study.
   Provides a critical review of the literature.
The framework developed for Australia in this
publication can be used elsewhere.

87. Freund, B. **The African Worker**. Cambridge:
      Cambridge University Press, 1988.

   Provides a synthesis of issues and debates
from the work of writers in various disciplines on
labor history and labor studies in Africa.
Considers the development of critical literature
on the issue. Contains biographical essays and a
bibliography which gives readers interested more
detail on particular regions or issues.
A very useful reference book on African labor.

88. Friedman, D.E. "Child Care for Employees' Kids."
      Harvard Business Review, 64(2) 1986, 26.

   Provides a positive view of employer-
supported child care. Management can gain in
several ways: lower turnover, less absenteeism,
fewer errors and accidents. There would be a rise
in productivity, attendance would improve and
workers would be happier. Gives update on what
corporations are doing, and provides cost-benefits
and options available.
   Illuminating, and a must reading for
prospective managers.

89. Gorman, J. **To Build Jerusalem: A Photographic
      Remembrance of Working Class Life, 1875-1950.**
      London: Scorpion Publications, 1980.

   Provides a history of working people and the
changes in their lives over the last century,
through a collection of extraordinary photographs
that have been collected from a wide range of
sources and are accompanied by an informative
commentary. The working class lived, played, and
struggled as they built the labor movement.

An innovative manner of presenting the
history of workers. Of interest to academics,
unions, workers and the general public.

90. Green, J.K. **The World of the Worker: Labour in
        Twentieth Century America.** Toronto: McGraw-
        Hill Ryerson Ltd., 1980.

    Provides a synthesis of the literature on
workers' experience in America, incorporating the
work place, union, community, strike, changes in
technology and political activism. The discussion
goes beyond the house of labor to the wider world
of the workers. More importantly, it traces the
implication of the growing participation of women
in the labor market, and the great exodus of black
people from the rural south to the industrial
cities of the north, for working class life in
this century.
    A remarkable book for anyone who seeks an
introduction to the social history of 20th century
America.

(A rejoinder to Item 27)

91. Greenberger, E. and L. Steinberg **When Teenagers
        Work: The Psychological and Social Costs of
        Adolescent Employment.** New York: Basic Books,
        1986.

    Teenage employment outpaced all projected
trends and what is needed is a comprehension
of the quality of this adolescent experience and
its contribution to personal development. While
in the not-too-far distant past enrollment in
school precluded labor market activity, for most
youngsters today work and education are combined.
Factors accounting for the growing participation
of youth in the labor market are discussed and it
is shown that the typical work place is age-
segregated, uninspiring and involves repetitive
tasks over which they have little control.
    A thought provoking book which offers helpful
ideas for research and policy analysis.

(A rejoinder to Item 165)

92. Hamermesh, D.S. **Labour in the Public and Nonprofit Sectors**, New Jersey: Princeton University Press, 1975.

    Since World War II, the government's share of total expenditure and employment has increased dramatically. As well, the number of unions in the public sector has increased in a striking manner. This study focuses on the employment problems in the public sector, and discusses how the employment and wage determination differ between the profit-making industry and the rest of the economy. It also deals with the effects of wage subsidies and general revenue sharing on public employment, and examines what determines variations in strike activities in the public sector.
    A new approach by economists, of particular use to policy makers.

93. Handy, C. **The Future of Work.** Oxford: Basil Blackwell, 1984.

    The message is that there can be no looking back. The new patterns of work are on their way whether we welcome them or not. Discusses new forms of work in the future: part-time work and shorter careers, voluntary and co-operative work, possibilities for self-employment, contract work, and organizing work in Japanese style.
    Provides a necessary point of departure for a debate which cannot be postponed while the individual and society have to face sweeping changes regarding work.

94. Haraszti, M. **A Worker in a Worker's State: Piece-rates in Hungary** (translated by M. Wright). New York: Universe Books in Association with New Left Review. 1977.

Describes the social relations in a Hungarian factory. The kind of social relations and economic goals described here are a classic description of a capitalist society--whether the property is owned by individuals, corporations, or even the state. Covers a wide range of topics: control, safety, participation, sabotage and frustrations. Points to the coercion, manipulation and lack of control that workers face, the hostility towards the system that permeates the workers' lives, and the subtle, but devastating forms of resistance.

An important and beautifully written account of the daily lives of workers in Hungary, and a savage attack on capitalism.

95. Harrison, J.F.C. **The Common People**. London: Flamingo, 1984.

Aims to describe the everyday life of ordinary people--their work, family relationships, social structures, ideas and beliefs, institutions, and movements. To accomplish this task, this book draws upon a wide variety of recent work done in popular religions, cultural change, the history of women, family and demography. The result is a vivid history of the past as experienced by common people--peasants, artisans and industrial workers.

An important piece of scholarship which enables us to trace the roots of our present history.

(A rejoinder to Items 101, 102)

96. Hobsbawn, E. **Worlds of Labour: Further Studies in the History of Labour**. London: Weidenfeld and Nicolson, 1984.

Presents a rigorous discussion and analysis of the history of working men and women between the late 18th and mid-20th centuries emphasizing the interrelation between the impact of labor organizations, policies and ideas, and the everyday life of working people. Makes it clear

that the history of the working class cannot be
written in isolation from the other classes, and
from the states, institutions, ideas, and
transformation of the economies.
   A complex historical process is expressed in
clear prose by the world's leading labor
historian. A valuable source of reference for
those interested in this subject.

97. Jencks, C., L. Perman, and L. Rainwater. "What is
       a Good Job? A New Measure of Labour Market
       Success." **American Journal of Sociology**,
       93(6) 1988, 1322-57.

       Constructs an index of job desirability.
   Weighs 13 job characteristics according to their
   effects on workers' judgments, and about how good
   their jobs are compared with an average job.
   Earnings remain to be the single most determinant
   of a job's desirability.
       A useful index, which is able to explain the
   effects of sex, race and educational attainment on
   job rating.

98. Johnson, W.B. and A.H. Packer. **Work-place 2000:
       Work and Workers for the Twenty-first
       Century**. Indiana: Hudson Institute, 1987.

       Documents labor market trends in the United
   States, and makes a number of predictions about
   the future structure of the economy, labor force
   participation and the skill-level of workers.
       Can be used to understand the challenge of
   the emerging economy and evaluate the adequacy of
   our current policy.

99. Kaplinsky, R. **Micro-electronics and Employment
       Revisited: A Review**. Geneva: ILO, 1987.

       Critically reviews the theoretical and
   empirical writings on the impact of micro-
   technology on employment in both developed and
   developing countries. Examines the possibilities

for developing countries to advance their own
electronic industry. Concludes that in
industrialized countries the development of micro-
technology has been rapid, but uneven; levels of
unemployment, contrary to common belief, are
likely to decline in the long-term; the shift to a
new techno-economic paradigm seems to be
associated with a change in the organization of
work; and the new technology appears to be limited
to a number of newly industrializing countries.

Looks at direct, indirect, positive and
negative impacts of technology. Provides useful
information on both developed and developing
countries.

(A rejoinder to Items 237, 240, 253)

100. Krahn, H.J., and S.L. Lowe. **Work, Industry and
        Canadian Society.** Scarborough, Ontario:
        Nelson Canada, 1988.

Examines a wide range of questions about the
changing nature and context of work and the
effects of different types of work arrangements
for the individual and society. Among the issues
discussed at length are: industrialization and the
rise of capitalism; the major trend in the
development of the labor force; labor market and
organizational theories; the transformation in
women's economic role; and the controversial areas
of unions, industrial conflict and strikes.

A suitable textbook for an undergraduate
course on industrial sociology.

(A rejoinder to Items 112, 126)

* Kraut, R.E. (Item 248)

101. Lane, D. and E. O'Dell. **The Soviet Industrial
        Worker.** New York: St. Martin's Press, 1978.

Examines working class cleavages in a society
with different property and class relations. In
Britain, conflict with management and the State is
institutionally organized, whereas, in the Soviet

Union, workers are incorporated by the school, factory, union, management and the communist party. As well, the working class in the Soviet Union is more stratified than in the west.

Brings together a whole range of research done by Soviet sociologists, and is valuable for comparative purposes.

(A rejoinder to Items 95, 102)

102. LeMasters, E.E. **Blue Collar Aristocrats: Life-Styles at a Working Class Tavern**, Wisconsin: The University of Wisconsin Press, 1975.

Employs the method of participant observation, and discusses the life style of blue-collar workers. Describes, in simple language, various aspects of working people's lives: their families, churches, ideas, marriages, work, communities, race and politics.

A valuable contribution to the ethnography of American Society.

(A rejoinder to Items 59, 95, 101)

103. Miller, A.R., D.J. Treiman, P.S. Cain, and P.A. Rose. **Work, Jobs and Occupations: A Critical Review of the Dictionary of Occupational Titles.** Washington, D.C.: National Academy Press, 1980.

The Dictionary of Occupational Titles (DOT) provides definitions for over 12,000 occupations, and serves as a major source for an occupational classification system. The main criticism of DOT is that it contains some sex bias, over-represents jobs in manufacturing and production industries, and under-represents jobs in retail, trade and service industries.

A required reading for anybody who uses DOT.

(A rejoinder to Item 78)

104. Newman, K.S. **Falling From Grace: The Experience**
     of Downward Mobility in the American Middle
     Class. New York: Free Press, 1988.

     Written from the perspective of an
     anthropologist, this work employs qualitative
     methods and examines intra-generational downward
     mobility. The groups under study include skidding
     white collar business executives, air traffic
     controllers, blue collar workers, and divorced
     women. Looks at the causes and types of downward
     mobility. Although each of these groups are
     different, there are some common elements among
     them, i.e. all of them have felt anger and a
     strong sense of betrayal, and their self-worth has
     been called into question.
     An excellent treatment of a neglected aspect
     of mobility.

     * *Pahl, R.E. (Item 12)*

105. Patrick, H. with the assistance of L. Meissner.
     Japanese Industrialization and Its Social
     Consequences. Berkeley: University of
     California Press, 1976.

     Examines some important aspects of Japanese
     industrial relations and their effects on social
     change, from the mid-19th century to the present.
     Provides a discussion of three intertwined major
     issues: sociological and economic characteristics
     of industrial workers in Japan; the micro-pattern
     of industrial development, and questions
     associated with certain features of industrial
     firms; and the major social impact of industrial
     development.
     Of particular value is the adoption of
     comparative methodology and the inclusion in each
     essay of an extensive bibliography.

     (A rejoinder to Items 47, 66)

106. Peace, W.H. "I Thought I Knew What Good Management
     Was." **Harvard Business Review**, 64(2) 1986,
     59.

Reviews the experience of one successful
manager and stresses that it is not enough to have
well-defined goals, tasks and priorities.
Traditional channels of communication are
inefficient. It is essential to build trust and
have open face-to-face communication with
employees.
Provides evidence for the importance of human
relations in today's management.

107. Plath, D.W. (ed.). **Work and Lifecourse in Japan**,
Albany: State University of New York Press,
1983.

Questions misleading western images of work
in Japan, showing that Japanese work-life is no
better than that in other industrial nations.
Like workers anywhere, they have to go through
life reconciling their obligation to their job
with their duties to family, community and
personal needs. Here, we learn about life and
work in Japan from a worker's point of view.
This book has significance for the study of
Japanese ethnology and for our understanding of
life in mass societies.

(A rejoinder to Items 117, 130, 151, 193)

108. Purcell, K., S. Wood, A. Watson and S. Allan
(eds.). **The Changing Experience of
Employment**. London: Macmillan, 1986.

Discusses detailed case studies of different
occupations, ranging from managers, through
routine white-collar workers, to skilled manual
workers and low-paid marginalized female workers.
Describes the uneven impact of micro-technology
and the erosion of middle managers.
This collection of essays is evidence of the
current trend against generalization regarding
work.

109. Rau, W.C., D.W. Roncek. "Labor Force
     Transformations among Seven Major Industrial
     Nations, 1920-1970." **Social Science
     Quarterly**, 68(2) 1987, 326-339.

     Reanalyses labor force statistics from the
     United States, Canada, England, Germany, France,
     Italy and Japan. Suggests that the service sector
     must be disaggregated, as the services have very
     different growth patterns.
     Provides a useful picture of the trends in
     the labor force in industrialized countries.

110. Richards, A. and P.L. Martin (ed.). **Migration
     Mechanization and Agricultural Labour Markets
     in Eygpt**. Cairo: The American University in
     Cairo Press, 1983.

     Presents the major strands of the debate on
     the issue of labor shortage or surplus in Egyptian
     agriculture. Sees a need to examine the
     implications of both mechanization and migration
     for rural and urban labor markets. This
     interdependence cannot be ignored in Egypt or any
     other Third World country.
     Many of the questions raised here are crucial
     for understanding development and employment
     problems in Third World countries.

111. Riddel, W.C. (ed.). **Work and Pay: The Canadian
     Labour Market**. Toronto: University of
     Toronto Press, 1985.

     Discusses the major labor market changes and
     trends observed in Canada over the decades,
     including the rise in female labor force
     participation, the increase in unemployment, the
     growth in two-income earner families, the growing
     importance of part-time work, the decline in real
     earnings, and increasing government involvement in
     the economy.
     A useful source for policy makers and
     students of industrial relations. Raises many
     issues which concern researchers and policy
     makers in industrial countries.

112. Ritzer, G. and D. Walczak. **Working: Conflict and Change**, Third edition, New Jersey: Prentice-Hall, 1986.

    This publication reflects the dramatic changes in the world of work given the passage of nine years since the second edition of this book. Provides a sociological analysis of work in contemporary America, focusing on the changing nature of occupations and careers that individuals experience in their work lives. Examines the efforts and mechanisms that people use to cope with conflicts which exist in the world of work.
    Can serve as a basic text for an undergraduate course in the sociology of work and occupations.

    (A rejoinder to Items 100, 126)

113. Robischon, M.M., B.C. Levine and M. Glaberman. **Work and Society**. Detroit, Michigan: Wayne State University Press, 1977.

    Contains some of the best material on the importance of work in defining the nature of social relations and provides an explanation for the transition from feudalism to capitalism, and the specific changes associated with it. Analyses the shift from monopoly capitalism to welfare capitalism, the working class and their problems, working class organization, and the internal dynamics and policies of unions.
    A valuable addition to the literature on the historical transformation of work in the west.

114. Rosenbaum, J.E. and T. Kariya. "From High School to Work: Market and Institutional Mechanisms in Japan." **American Journal of Sociology**, 94(6) 1989, 1334-1365.

    Measures the ties between Japanese schools and employers. Many Japanese schools have an agreement with employers to find jobs for their students. Shows that the Japanese shift the

competition for jobs from the labor market into
the schools. This linkage between the schools and
employers differs from the economic market model
and personal network model in other countries.
   Sheds light on an important mechanism of
employment in Japan. A very useful source for
comparative purposes.

115. Rothwell, R. and W. Zegvels. **Technical Change and
       Employment**. New York: St. Martin's Press,
       1980.

       Deals with six countries' policies toward
technological innovation in industry: Canada,
France, West Germany, the Netherlands, Ireland and
the United Kingdom. Assesses the employment
impact of certain technological changes in
industry, and shows that manufacturing in the
countries that were first to industrialize is no
longer a direct source of job creation and that
tertiary sectors will shortly reach the limit of
their capacity to absorb the growth of the labor
force. Advises the governments to develop
policies that will encourage the development of
new products to come from small firms.
   Has a rich account of technological and
employment trends in some important industries.

116. Samorodov, A. "Coping with the Employment Effects
       of Restructuring in Eastern Europe."
       International Labour Review, 28(3) 1989, 357-
       372.

       Economic reforms in socialist countries of
Eastern Europe gave a radical boost to the
independence of enterprises. Micro-electronic
technologies are being introduced to increase
labor productivity and these changes and 'their
impact on employment are discussed. The focus is
on training, retraining and re-employment of
released workers. As full employment remains the
principle of the system, numerous adjustments in
different areas are required.
   A good piece of work on the recent factors
affecting employment strategies in Eastern Europe.

117. Shirai, T. (ed.). **Contemporary Industrial Relations in Japan**. Wisconsin: Wisconsin University Press, 1983.

Questions the stereotyped treatment of work and industry in Japan put forward by the mass media and popular literature written outside of Japan. Brings out the distinctive peculiarities of the Japanese style of labor relations. Includes several important works in which insightful observations and analysis of the subject stimulated lively discussions among Japanese scholars and policy makers about the need to re-examine Japanese industrial relations.

Provides the foreign audience with enough relevant information to facilitate a good understanding of the complexity of the industrial relations system in contemporary Japan.

(A rejoinder to Items 107, 130, 151)

118. Shirley, S. (Interview by E.G.C. Collins) "A Company Without Office." **Harvard Business Review**, 64(1) 1986, 127.

An international computer consulting company hires over 1,000 workers in three countries, but no one goes to the office. The director talks about issues relating to the nature and organization of work in this vision of the future office.

Relevant for the discussion on the impact of technology and the future of work.

* *Shlapentokh, V. (Item 15)*

119. Siegel, D. "The Changing Shape and Nature of Public Service Employment." **Canadian Public Administration**, 31(2) 1988, 159-193.

Provides a quantitative overview of international trends in employment in the public sector. Analyses these trends and identifies

political and management consequences which follow
from them.
　　Helps to understand the changing nature of
the labor force in industrialized countries.

120. Singlemann, J. **From Agriculture to Services: The
　　　Transformation of Industrial Employment.**
　　　Beverly Hills: Sage Publications, 1978.

　　　Addresses a central trend in advanced
industrialized countries: the shift from
agriculture to manufacturing.　　Examines the
patterns of this transformation during the 20th
century in the United States, Canada, Great
Britain, West Germany, France, Italy and Japan.
Also discusses some of the sociological
consequences of this transformation of employment,
such as changes in the occupational structure, the
nature of work, the class structure, and
international migration.
　　Provides detailed information on the service
industry.　　Useful for anyone interested in
understanding the pattern of change in employment
in industrialized countries.

121. Stewart, A., K. Prandy and R.M. Blackburn. **Social
　　　Stratification and Occupations**, London:
　　　Macmillan Press Ltd, 1980.

　　　Shows that the relationships between
occupation and stratification are more complex
than has been supposed and challenges the
assumption that occupations, as conventionally
defined, can be used as indicators of class or
status position.　　The structure of social
inequality is shown to be more coherent and stable
than has generally been believed. .
　　An important contribution for understanding
the social reproduction of inequality.

122. Trager, L. "A Re-examination of the Urban Informal
　　　Sector in West Africa." **Canadian Journal of
　　　African Studies**, 21(2) 1987, 238-255.

This discussion encompasses the diversity of informal sector activities, and includes both self-employed or non-wage workers, as well as those employed below minimum wage and with no social security. Provides directions for future research.

Essential for understanding the nature of the economy and market in the developing countries.

123. Triska, J.F. and C. Gati. **Blue Collar Workers in Eastern Europe**. London: George Allen and Unwin, 1981.

Discusses the role, economic condition, attitude, social and demographic characteristics and political involvement of the East European working class, and uses a number of case studies to describe the problems which confront it. Shows that East European governments are hesitant to use force, yet they lack the economic means to meet workers' demands. Also examines the policy implications of these workers' new assertiveness.

Of particular use to those interested in labor unions, workers' councils and socialist management.

124. Vanackere, M. "Conditions of Agricultural Day Labourers in Mexico." **International Labour Review**, 127(1) 1988, 91-110.

Provides an account of how agricultural day workers are hired, the type of work they do, and how they are paid. Day laborers do not enjoy the protective measures which covers Mexican workers in general. Unfortunately, these workers are scattered geographically, and hard to organize, and are unaware of their rights. Poverty is their lot.

Although it focuses on Mexico, this discussion is applicable to other developing countries.

125. Vasegh-Daneshvary, N., M. Scholttmann, H.W.
         Herzog, Jr. "Immigration of Engineers,
         Scientists, and Physicians and the U.S. High
         Technology Renaissance." **Social Science
         Quarterly**, 68(2) 1987, 311-325.

         Examines the importance of the immigration of
a high-technology and medical work force for the
United States. Demonstrates the extent to which
professional workers from developing countries
have fueled the high-technology job growth in the
United States. Of course, the government's
immigration policy plays a central role in this
process.
         A contribution to the study of immigrant
labor, brain drain from developing countries, and
the composition of high-technology occupations in
the United States.

126. Watson, T.J. **Sociology, Work and Industry**.
         London: Routledge and Kegan Paul, 1980.

         Covers some of the major topics in the area
of sociology of work. Intends to provide a text
which can be useful to those specializing in
industrial sociology, as well as those who have an
interest in the area of work.

(A rejoinder to 100, 112)

127. Wilkes, J. (ed.). **The Future of Work**. London:
         Allen and Unwin, 1981.

         Deals with a number of contemporary themes:
the impact of technology on employment; the
relation between work roles and individual
identity; methods of coping with a shortage of
work; the plight of the chronically unemployed;
permanent part-time jobs; and the development of
managerial practices since the industrial
revolution.
         Provides a good review of contemporary
measures available for employment policies.

128. Willis, P. **Learning to Labour**. London: Saxon
     House, 1977.

     Combines a sophisticated theoretical
     framework with an intensive ethnographic study of
     working class boys on their road from school to
     work. The cultural milieu in which these students
     have developed encourages them to choose working
     class jobs.
     A provocative 'discourse' analysis which
     shows the power of ideology in reproducing the
     occupational structure.

129. Wipper, A. (ed.). **The Sociology of Work**. Ottawa:
     Carleton University Press, 1984.

     Reviews changes in the Canadian labor force
     from 1901 to 1971 and covers the standard general
     topics in the sociology of work, such as:
     occupational recruitment, the bureaucratic nature
     of work, alienation, status and hierarchy at work,
     and the importance of gender and ethnicity.
     Provides a long list of readings, and can
     serve as an introductory text.

130. Woronoff, J. **Japan's Wasted Workers**. Tokyo: Lotus
     Press, 1983.

     As the world has become more interested in
     Japan's famous management style and is talking
     seriously of using it as a model, the Japanese have
     become disenchanted with it and are talking of a
     need for radical change. Woronoff looks at the
     less-than-model companies that make up the
     majority of corporate enterprises in Japan,
     addresses their major weaknesses and shows there
     is enough dissatisfaction in management and labor
     groups to call for implementing reforms.
     Provides original insight on female labor and
     white-collar workers. A required text for anyone
     interested in Japanese labor relations.

     (A rejoinder to Items 107, 117, 151)

CHAPTER TWO

THE DIVISION OF LABOR

Labor Market Segmentation:
Cleavages among Workers

131. Abella, I.M. and D. Millar, **The Canadian Worker in the Twentieth Century**. Toronto: Oxford University Press, 1978.

Covers the period between 1900-1940 and tries to reconstruct the daily lives of the men, women and children who helped to build this nation. Fulfills this purpose by a careful use of memories, interviews, letters, articles, speeches and testimonies. Shows clearly that in the process of industrialization in Canada, immigrant workers bore an inequitable burden. Exploitation characterized the nature of work for the cheap immigrant workers. Makes it clear that this hardship was not just the feature of the bad old order, but that the brutal exploitation of low-status immigrants continues today.
A valuable study which deserves a wide readership.

132. Bequele, A. and Boyden, J. "Working Children: Current Trends and Policy Responses." **International Labour Review**, 127(2) 1988, 153-172.

Examines the types of employment children are engaged in, the risks to which they are exposed, the relationship between work and schooling, and the constraint on the exercise of their rights. Children are employed in a great variety of jobs, and many are trapped in highly exploitative and abusive employment relationships. Provides examples of initiatives which have been helpful in protecting child workers.
An important addition to the literature on work in developing countries.

(A rejoinder to Items 162, 171)

133. Borjas, G.J.   "Immigrants, Minorities, and Labour
       Market Competition." **Industrial and Labour
       Relations Review,**   40(3) 1987, 382-392.

        Examines labor market competition among
immigrants, minorities and the native population.
Shows that immigrants are a substitute for some
groups of labor and complement others.   In
general, the shift in immigrant supply does not
have much effect on the earnings of native-born
men.   However, increases in the supply of
immigrants have a large impact on the earnings of
the immigrants themselves.
        An illuminating addition to the literature on
a segmented labor market.

134. Brewer, R.M.   "Black Women in Poverty: Some
       Comments on Female-Headed Families." **Signs,**
       13(2) 1988, 331-339.

        Puts the current debate on poor black women
heading households within a structural and
political-economic context, and shows that
theories centered in the human capital deficit
notion--lack of training, education or skills--are
inadequate for explaining the poverty of female-
headed families.   Places the emphasis on the
analysis of changes in the family structure within
the context of an industrial capitalist system and
its welfare-state practices.   The realities of the
gender and race-based operation of the labor force
challenges the human capital approach to women's
poverty.
        An excellent example of the segmentation
found in the labor market.

135. Bromley, R. and C. Gerry (eds.), **Casual Work and
       Poverty in Third World Cities.**   New York:
       John Wiley, 1979.

        Brings together under the general title of
'casual poor' research on urban poverty and its
relation to the labor process.   This contribution
comprises both conceptual and descriptive articles

and draws materials from Latin America, Africa and Asia, covering a diversity of work experiences.

Can be a valuable source of reference, and attractive to those concerned with the issue of work and the 'working poor' in the developing countries.

136. Buechler, H.C. and Buechler, J.M. **Migrants in Europe: The Role of Family, Labour and Politics.** Westport: Greenwood, 1987.

The migration process is seen as embedded in historical circumstances that determine the size and shape of labor outflows. Stresses the importance of illegal immigration to and employment in Germany in the early 1970's. Correctly draws attention to the often overlooked role played by migrant women, many of whom did not go to Germany as spouses or dependents.

Enables readers to grasp the complexity of the lives of immigrants, their problems and their responses to new environments.

(A rejoinder to Items 164, 172)

137. Burkhauser, R.V. and R.H. Haveman. **Disability and Work: The Economy of American Policy.** Baltimore The Johns Hopkins University Press, 1982.

Draws on the existing body of research, and provides a background on the structure and impact of U.S. disability policy-related income support programs and other programs targeted at disabled workers. It describes the disabled working population on which the analysis focuses, showing that this population is concentrated in the older age categories, the black people, and the groups with less education. It also reviews the complex sets of programs which provide assistance to disabled workers, and addresses a few of the fundamental issues surrounding disability policy.

The information provided by this volume would be of value to any participant in policy debate and to disabled workers.

(A rejoinder to Item 146)

138. Casey, B. and Bruche, G. **Work or Retirement?**
     Labour Market and Social Policy for Older
     Workers in France, Britain, the Netherlands,
     Sweden and the U.S.A. Brookfield, VT.:
     Gower, 1983.

          Reviews policies for older workers still
     employed and those experiencing long-term
     unemployment. Shows that adjusting work places to
     the needs of an aging work force is low in the
     priorities of most employers. As well, the main
     thrust of labor policy has been towards the
     exclusion of older people from paid work. This
     has been accompanied by the provision of a variety
     of types of income support, even though the
     generosity of these schemes is subject to
     discrepancy.
          An extremely valuable source. Provides
     useful summaries of a range of policies affecting
     older workers in five countries.

139. Castels, S. and G. Kosack. **Immigrant Workers and**
     Class Structure in Western Europe. 2nd
     edition. Oxford: Oxford University Press,
     1985.

          This second edition broadens the theme of the
     first, and provides an international perspective
     of the mass movement of workers from Southern
     Europe and the Third World to the expanding
     economies of Western Europe during the post-war
     period. It looks at the way immigrants were
     received, their lives, and their position in the
     recipient countries. The effect of emigration on
     the sending countries is also examined. It is
     shown that the shift from economic expansion to
     long-term stagnation has affected immigrant
     workers; the trend has been towards political and
     cultural separatism and the growth of racism.
          An authoritative source for understanding the
     position of immigrant workers.

140. Cohen, R. **The New Helots: Migrants in the International Division of Labor.** Brookfield, VT.: Gower, 1987.

Criticizes the Marxian claim that the free worker is central to the capitalist mode of production. Shows that, throughout its history, capitalism has relied on a combination of labor regimes. Capitalism has found new ways of incorporating migrant workers and using them to maintain the elasticity of the work force, keep wages down and create divisions. Provides evidence from undocumented workers from Mexico, legal temporary workers from the Caribbean in United States agriculture, 'guest workers' in Western Europe, and looks at the way South Africa has been recruiting workers from neighboring countries.
Contains abundant fascinating details and is a must for those interested in the division of labor in contemporary capitalism.

141. Doering, M., S.R. Rhodes, M. Schuster. **The Aging Worker: Research and Recommendations.** Beverly Hills: Sage Publications, 1983.

Discusses a number of important issues relating to the psychological characteristics of the older worker: job satisfaction, work involvement, organizational commitment and work accidents. Contains interesting information on the management of an aging work force and provides an extensive summary of studies on the aging worker.
Well-designed and documented; of interest to policy makers, planners, managers, and academics. The Appendix is particularly useful for researchers beginning to delve into the study of aging workers.

142. Fevre, R. **Cheap Labour and Racial Discrimination.** Aldershot: Gower, 1984.

Uses the case of the wool industry and shows
that post-war changes made many of the semi and
unskilled jobs in the industry unattractive to
white English workers. Asians were the only ones
prepared to work in the industry. However, with
the current restructuring of the industry, there
is every reason to believe that black workers
will be squeezed out of the labor market entirely.
A valuable detailed study of black people in
the textile industry. Incorporates the advances
of recent work on the labor process into the
analysis of racial discrimination in employment.

143. First, R. **Black Gold: The Mozambican Miner,
      Proletarian and Peasant**. Brighton, Sussex:
      Harvester Press, 1983.

Analyses the way in which cheap, politically
subordinated labor provided the engine for capital
accumulation and became the material basis for
apartheid. Focuses on Mozambique, one of the
major labor exporting areas. The most important
message is the complementarity of the peasant
economy with the extraction of gold and coal by
mining capital.
It is based on many extensive interviews with
returned miners and the peasantry. Another
important addition to the sociology of work and
discrimination.

144. Gunatilleke, G. **Migration of Asian Workers to the
      Arab World**. Tokyo: The United Nations
      University, 1986.

Surveys the present state of the art on the
migration of Asian workers to the Middle East.
Reviews and evaluates Asian policies which deal
with migration issues and shows that labor
migration has had far reaching socioeconomic,
cultural and demographic consequences.
The detailed information on migrant labor,
and the comparative view launched here are of
value for policy makers and students of
international labor migration.

145. Hakim, C. **Home-based Work in Britain: A Report on the National Home-working Survey and DE Research Program on Homework.** London: Department of Employment Research, Paper No. 60, 1987.

Dispels many myths about contemporary home-workers in Britain. Home-workers are not predominantly found in the industrial sector, nor are they disproportionately unskilled. Home-based work is equally divided between men and women. However, those working at home are mainly female, while those working from home tend to be men.
Provides an important empirical basis for policy makers and researchers in advanced industrialized countries.

(A rejoinder to Items 149, 181)

146. Harper, M. and W. Momm. **Self-employment for Disabled Persons: Experiences from Africa and Asia.** Geneva: International Labour Office, 1989.

Examines what disabled people can achieve as entrepreneurs and looks at self-employment as an employment option. Highlights the success and problems of self-employment among disabled people. Also questions the conventional assumptions about disability and provides encouragement to disabled entrepreneurs and institutions that serve them.
Designed to promote self-help and economic self-reliance for disabled people. Offers valuable advice to planners and rehabilitation professionals.

(A rejoinder to Item 137)

147. Holmstrom, M. **Industry and Inequality: The Social Anthropology of Indian Labour.** Cambridge: Cambridge University Press, 1984.

Covers a wide range of topics relating to industrial work relations. Describes the inter-

relationships of different types of enterprises
and the systematic differences between permanent
wage-workers, contract workers and casual workers.
The conclusion is that organized and unorganized
workers act as separate classes.

Provides a major synthesis of the literature
on Indian Industrial labor.

148. Hyman, R. and R. Price (eds.). **The New Working
     Class? White Collar Workers and Their
     Organizations.** London: Macmillan Press,
     1983.

     Examines the class position of white-collar
workers and the trend towards unionization among
them. Presents the central debate on the nature
of white-collar unionism, and discusses the
differences and similarities of white-collar
unions with those of traditional unions. Includes
contributions from well-known authors, such as
Braverman, Gorz, Mandel, Giddens, Lockwood, Mills,
Galbraith, Poulantzas and Wright.

Useful as a scholarly source and as a set of
readings on white-collar unionism.

149. Johnson, L.C., with R. E. Johnson. **The Seam
     Allowance: Industrial Home Sewing in Canada.**
     Toronto: The Women's Press, 1982.

     Uncovers the fact that women of the
sweatshops are a hidden labor force. They work
long hours in crowded rooms, earn less than
minimum wage, and often work for marginal
employers. They are not a shadow from the past,
but are here today in one of Canada's largest
cities.

While the focus is limited to Toronto, it is
representative of workers in the clothing industry
elsewhere and of crucial value for understanding a
segmented labor market.

(A rejoinder to Items 145, 181, 197, 229)

150. Jones, E. W. "Black Managers: The Dream Deferred."
     Harvard Business Review, 64(3) 1986, 84.

     Many blacks hold positions of responsibility
     with prestige and income. However, many are
     disillusioned about their chances for ultimate
     success. They find themselves stalled in the rank
     of junior executives, dismayed that they have not
     gained acceptance on a par with their white peers.
     Introduces the frustrations and pains of some
     of the best black managers. Essential for
     understanding the effects of racism in the labor
     market.

151. Kamata, S. **Japan In the Passing Lane: An
     Insider's Account of Life in a Japanese Auto
     Industry.** New York: Pantheon Books, 1982.

     A straightforward, powerful insider's view of
     the seasonal workers' daily life in an auto
     industry in Japan. Questions the inhumanity of
     assembly line production and provides a vivid
     description of the dark side of a factory life in
     Japan. The views expressed here are opposite to
     the stereotyped image of Japanese industrial work,
     featuring guarantee of lifetime employment,
     joyful company songs, group exercises and the
     spirit of Zen.
     Provides a stunning account of how the
     miracle of the Japanese auto industry was
     accomplished. A must for students of Japanese
     industrial relations.

     (A rejoinder to Items 107, 117, 130)

152. Koch, J.V. "The Incomes of Recent Immigrants: A
     Look at Ethnic Differences." **Social Science
     Quarterly,** 68(2) 1987, 294-310.

     Recent immigrants to the United States are
     predominantly Asian and Hispanic in origin, and
     are better educated than previous immigrants.
     Discusses the great diversity among recent

immigrants, in terms of their human capital and
demographic characteristics.
Provides insights for understanding the
immigrants' position in the labor market.

153. Lemoine, M. **Bitter-Sugar: Slaves Today in the
     Caribbean**. Chicago: Banner Press, 1981.

A powerful documentary about one of the most
tragic processes of human exploitation in the
world today. It deals with the plight of Haitian
workers who sign temporary labor contracts to work
on the sugar plantation in the Dominican Republic.
A successful integration of moving literary
narrative and objective journalism. A must for
anyone interested in the study of Third World
labor.

(A rejoinder to Item 157)

154. Letkemann, P. **Crime as Work**. Englewood Cliffs:
     Prentice-Hall, 1973.

Examines in detail the social and technical
organization of two criminal activities--
safecracking and bank robbing--emphasizing their
occupational aspects. The major question is "How
did you go about committing such-and-such a
criminal act?" Finds out about the activities,
the organization, the tools used and the potential
of the jobs. Discusses the specific work demands
and work-related contingencies of specific
criminal activities.
An insightful and interesting study of
working illegally.

(A rejoinder to Item 176)

155. Levitan, S. A. and I. Shapiro. **Working, But Poor:
     America's Contradiction**. Baltimore: Johns
     Hopkins University Press, 1987.

Describes the life of families below the official poverty line, people who work full-time, year-round, and live in poor families. Identifies the working poor by age, sex and race. Reviews an array of public programs that might improve the earnings of the working poor, but calls attention to the reality that many American workers cannot earn enough to bring their families out of poverty.

An essential study for policy makers and those interested in labor market studies.

156. Littler, C. R. and G. Salaman. **Class at Work: The Design, Allocation and Control of Jobs.** London: Batsford Academic and Educational Ltd., 1984.

Discusses the existence of systematic inequalities in the work place. Exploitation is the direct product of fundamental class divisions which exist between employers and employees. Despite experimentation with other types of work, the division between management and workers is becoming strengthened. Employers are achieving this through technical, bureaucratic and ideological means.

Highlights the existing fundamental divisions in the work place in advanced industrialized countries.

(A rejoinder to Item 51)

157. Majka, L.C. and T.J. Majka. **Farm Workers, Agribusiness, and the State.** Philadelphia: Temple University Press, 1982.

Discusses the role of the state in the creation and maintenance of the 'Bracero Program', which ensures that agribusiness has access to a sufficient amount of cheap labor. Provides an excellent account of the formation of agricultural unions and labor militancy.

An important addition to the study of work relations in United States agriculture.

(A rejoinder to Items 157, 220)

158. Marshall, A. "Immigrant Workers in the Labour
        Market: A Comparative Analysis."
        International Social Science Journal, 36(101)
        1987, 501-518.

        Discusses the relationship between immigrants
     and the receiving labor market. Examines the
     allocation of immigrant labor in a number of
     countries, with a focus on activities that
     disproportionately employ foreign workers.
     Sheds light on factors that influence the
     distribution and mobility of immigrant workers in
     the employment structure.
        An important piece for understanding the
     nature of a segmented labor market.

159. Massey, D. Spatial Divisions of Labour: Social
        Structures and the Geography of Production.
        London: Macmillan, 1984.

        Looks at some of the ramifications of the
     spatial organization of production. The thesis is
     that behind major shifts ¦ among ¦ dominant spatial
     divisions of labor within a country lie changes in
     the spatial organization of capitalist relations
     of production. Provides a new approach to the
     conceptualization of the geography of industry.
        Helps to understand why different groups in
     society and different parts of the social
     structure have particular geographic distribution.
     Important for students of industrial geography.

160. McTaggart Almquist, E. Minorities, Gender and
        Work. Lexington, Mass.: Lexington Books,
        1979.

        Looks at the historical and social factors
     which determine the occupational structure of the
     above groups, the part played by race and the cost
     of labor force discrimination. Discusses the
     role of the government in the experience of

minorities in the labor market. Recognizes the diversity among women and shows that women cannot be viewed as homogeneous.

A welcome addition to the literature, not only on minorities and the labor force, but on women and work.

* Mies, M. (Item 26)

161. Morales, R. "Transitional Labour: Undocumented Workers in the Los Angeles Automobile Industry." **International Migration Review**, 17(4) 1983, 570-596.

Examines the position of undocumented workers among basic manufacturing sectors in Los Angeles and suggests that such labor temporarily facilitates the downward transition among industries. This transitional labor is seen as part of a broad trend towards the erosion of the primary labor market.

Of important value to those concerned with the issues of industrial restructuring, a segmented labor market and immigrant workers.

(A rejoinder to Item 157)

162. Myers, W.E. "Urban Working Children: A Comparison of Four Surveys from South America." **International Labour Review**, 128(3) 1989, 321-335.

Primarily focuses on the working children in urban streets of Bolivia, Brazil, Paraguay and Peru. Discusses their work, families, education, needs and aspirations. What is striking is that these young workers are pre-adolescent, male, work long hours and carry heavy family responsibilities.

Of particular interest to policy makers and those interested in the study of work in developing countries.

(A rejoinder to Items 132, 171)

163. Nishikawa, S. (ed.). **The Labour Market in Japan:**
        Selected Readings. Tokyo: University of
        Tokyo Press, 1980.

        Covers a range of topics, such as labor
     migration and mobility, female labor force
     participation, working hours and productivity,
     economic return to post-secondary education,
     intra-firm structure, and the nature of union
     power. Provides a rigorous analysis of the labor
     market behavior of married women. There is also
     illuminating insight into a seniority-based intra-
     firm wage system.
        Provides valuable general knowledge essential
     for our understanding of the Japanese labor
     market.

164. O'Brian, P. "Continuity and Change in Germany's
        Treatment of Non-Germans." **International**
        Migration Review, 22(3) 1988, 109-134.

        Criticizes governmental approaches to
     immigrants in Germany. Provides a review of the
     discussions on non-Germans under various German
     regimes and discusses recent changes in the
     government policies which attempt to integrate
     foreigners.
        Provides insights and guides for a new
     direction of research on migrants in Germany.

     (A rejoinder to Items 136, 172)

     * *Ogunbameru, O.A. (Item 11)*

165. Osterman, P. **Getting Started: The Youth Labour**
        Market. Cambridge, Mass.: The MIT Press,
        1980.

        Shows that young people drift through an
     aimless sequence of temporary dead-end jobs in
     secondary labor markets. There is a high rate of
     turnover among young workers, and more
     importantly, the careers they ultimately enter
     appear to have little or no relationship to their
     previous job experiences.

A worthwhile study, it brings out the
existing inequalities in the labor market and has
significant policy implications.

(A rejoinder to Item 91)

166. Paine, S. **Exporting Workers: The Turkish case.**
Cambridge: Cambridge University Press, 1974.

The major questions addressed here are: how
is Turkey affected in selling Turkish workers;
what is the implication of the returning Turkish
workers for Turkey; how do Turkish workers fare in
Europe, especially in Germany; and how is Germany
affected?
Rich in data and full of insights. Will
appeal to those interested in migrant labor in
general, and Turkish labor in Germany in
particular.

167. Parker, S. **Work and Retirement.** London: George
Allen and Unwin, 1982.

Examines people's experience regarding
retirement in Britain and the United States and
rejects the contention that retirement is
generally a more demoralizing experience for men
than women. Shows that a sizeable minority of
older people continue to work after normal
retirement age, and many others would prefer to
work part-time if they had the opportunity.
Reviews a large amount of literature, and
provides much insight on the question of work and
older people.

168. Penn, R. and H. Scattergood. "Continuities and
Change in Skilled Work: A Comparison of Five
Paper Manufacturing Plants in the U.K.,
Australia and the USA." **The British Journal
of Sociology,** 39(1) 1988, 69-85.

Evaluates theories of skilled work, and
suggests that the distinction between skilled and

non-skilled work is fundamental in establishing
occupational differentiation in all plants.
Conflicts exist and are affected by the wider
sociopolitical environment.
   Of particular use to those interested in
comparative industrial sociology.

169. Phizacklea, A. (ed.). **One Way Ticket: Migration
        and Female Labour**. London: Routledge and
        Kegan Paul, 1983.

        Shows that since the 1950's migrant female
workers have fulfilled the need for low-paid, low-
skilled and highly insecure jobs in the formal and
informal sectors of the west European economy.
These women are seen as bearers of a triple
burden: as migrants, as women and as low-paid
workers. Analyses the class position of migrant
women, and links the discussion to the structural
changes in the world economy and the creation of
armies of female migrant labor in the Third World.
   An important source for understanding the
nature of a segmented market at the international
level.

170. Phizacklea, A. and R. Miles. **Labour and Racism**.
        London: Routledge and Kegan Paul, 1980.

        Addresses important questions about the place
of black migrant workers in the United Kingdom's
economy. Discusses the deteriorating position of
blacks in the labor market, and how blacks faced
racism in the trade union and were not supported
by them.
   A must reading for understanding the impact
of race on industrial relations.

171. Rathgeber, E.M. "Education and Employment in the
        Informal Sector: A Review of Some Recent
        African Research." **Canadian Journal of
        African Studies**, 22(2) 1988, 270-290.

Youth unemployment and underemployment have become a problem in many African societies. The formal sector of the economy cannot provide employment opportunities for the growing population. As a result, the importance of the informal sector has increased.

Although the focus is on African societies, it addresses common problems which exist in all developing countries.

172. Rist, R. C. **Guestworkers in Germany: The Prospect for Pluralism**. New York: Praeger Publishers, 1978.

Analyses the consequences of workers' migration from the economy of less developed countries to the Federal Republic of Germany, one of the major importers of foreign labor. Uses a multifaceted approach to present a picture of the social conditions of the 'guestworkers', and the way German government and society have responded to their presence.

It does not provide a review of the latest developments, but discusses well the situation of migrants in the Federal Republic of Germany.

(A rejoinder to Items 136, 164)

173. Sacks, M.P. **Work and Equality in Soviet Society: The Division of Labor by Age, Gender and Nationality**. New York: Praeger, 1982.

This is a study of the gender, nationality and age differences outside the agricultural sector in the Soviet Union between 1939 and 1970. It provides a discussion of the methodology used, the variation among the major nationality groups, and the differences among males and females within each group and each occupational category. It also examines the relative economic development of the Soviet Union, and the structure of non-agrarian employment associated with it.

An important addition to the study of stratification in Soviet society.

(A rejoinder to Item 211)

174. Serageldin, I. et al. **Manpower and International Labour Migration in the Middle East and North Africa.** New York: Published for the World Bank by Oxford University Press, 1983.

     Both states importing and exporting labor are becoming concerned about the nature and composition of this movement. While repatriation of earnings has benefited individual workers and their families, and increased the flow of consumer goods and foreign exchange within the countries, remittances have not made a major contribution to development.
     Of use to those interested in manpower planning and labor education.

     * *Southhall, R. (Item 371)*

175. Stichter, S. **Migrant Laborers.** Cambridge: Cambridge University Press, 1985.

     Adopts a political economy approach to the study of circular labor migration in East, West and Southern Africa. Reviews a wide range of literature, and addresses the controversies over the origin of migrancy and its effects on the rural economy. Describes the experience of migrant workers in various types of labor systems and sheds light on the women migrants' experience. A major concern is to document migrant workers' resistance and the conditions under which it develops.
     An excellent study, and a contribution to the study of African workers in particular, and labor migration in general.

     * *Thomas, R.J. (Item 73)*

176. Weiss, L. "Explaining the Underground Economy: State and Social Structure." **The British Journal of Sociology,** 38(2) 1987, 216-234.

Discusses the collective, organized aspects of clandestine production, which forms a central part of the underground economy. Challenges the assumption that 'off-the books' employment is either extensive or related to a crisis of capitalism and the state. Uses the case of Italy to discuss the conditions under which the clandestine economy can flourish.

Brings out new dimensions of the clandestine economy, and helps to better understand this little-studied sector of the economy.

(A rejoinder to Item 154)

177. Wilkinson, F. **The Dynamics of Labour Market Segmentation**. London: Academic Press, 1981.

Illustrates the change in the discussion of labor market segmentation, from an emphasis on explaining a fairly stable structure of pay and inequalities to an analysis of dynamic changes in the labor market. Underlines the importance of specific historical experiences and the complex interplay of economic and industrial factors in determining labor market segmentation. Despite a variation in experiences, general patterns are observable in all countries under study.

Brings to the attention of a wide audience an important range of works on labor markets which are being undertaken in different countries.

Women: The Other Division of Labor

178. Acton, J., P. Goldsmith, and B. Shepard (eds.),
     Women at Work: Ontario 1850-1930. Toronto:
     Canadian Women's Educational Press, 1974.

     Discusses various forms of women's gainful
     employment during this period of
     industrialization. Emphasizes that women were
     treated as a reserve army of labor and dismissed
     when their labor was no longer necessary. The
     perceived incompatibility between family life and
     work enabled working women to be exploited more
     easily. Despite problems, women worked, and in
     some circumstances, fought against their own
     exploitation.
     A valuable social history of women and work
     in Canada. Enlightening and full of historical
     details.

     (A rejoinder to Item 183)

179. Afshar, H. **Work and Ideology in the Third World**.
     New York: Tavistock Publications, 1985.

     Aims to probe the sources and consequences of
     discrimination against women in the labor market.
     Contends that religious, political and cultural
     ideas make women's work invisible by preserving
     wage differentials and maintaining women as a
     reserve army of cheap labor. Contributors look at
     various developing countries, and challenge
     assumptions about women and work.
     Has much to offer, brings out gender based
     inequality, and documents the way in which
     traditional values affect women's lives, even as
     societies experience rapid change.

     (A rejoinder to Item 203)

180. Ahmed, I. (ed.). **Technology and Rural Women:
     Conceptual and Empirical Issues**. London:
     George Allen and Unwin, 1985.

Discusses the condition of rural women as producers in developing countries, focusing especially on how these women are affected by technological change. Stresses that the position of women is poor, relative to men, by every measure. Technological change systematically worsens the position of women, and women often suffer doubly. Within the household their income is declining and with modernization they also experience a decline in their relative position in the household.

Demonstrates the severe limitations of the traditional approach and is of particular use for theoretical, statistical and policy formulation.

181. Allan, S. and C. Wolkowitz. **Home-working: Myths and Realities.** London: Macmillan, 1987.

Claims that home-working is one among many forms of disguised wage-labor which serves the interest of capitalist suppliers and reproduces the gender division of labor in the home and labor market. Refutes conventional assumptions about home-working, and discusses its advantage for sub-contractors and suppliers seeking to pass on various costs and risks to cheap, flexible, home-workers.

Although there remain questions regarding the representativeness and reliability of the data collected, this composition offers theoretical and political contributions to the sociological literature on the subject.

182. Anker, R. and C. Hein (eds.). **Sex Inequalities in Urban Employment in the Third World.** London: Macmillan, 1986.

Focuses on the inequalities between men and women in urban labor markets in various Third World countries, and highlights the discrepancy between employers' assumptions about women's lesser commitment to the labor force participation and their actual work histories. Emphasizes rightly the contrast between women's low participation in the formal sector and their high level of economic activity in the informal sector.

Uses a variety of theoretical approaches, and is definitely a valuable addition to the published material available on women's urban employment in Third World countries.

183. Armstrong, P. and H. Armstrong. **The Double Ghetto: Canadian Women and Their Segregated Work.** Toronto: McClelland and Stewart, 1978.

Documents the reasons for the segregation of Canadian women into low-paid and low-status occupations. Addresses the growing contradiction between the essentially unchanged nature of women's work and status in the labor market, and the changes that have taken place during the past thirty years in women's lives. These changes have forced upon women a perception of the injustice inherent in their segregation, and they are rebelling against it.

A valuable contribution to the growing volume of literature about Canadian women at work. An excellent list of references form a useful bibliography.

(A rejoinder to Items 178, 196, 205)

184. Beechey, V. **Unequal Work.** London: Verso, 1987.

Reviews the history of British feminist concerns from the 1960's to the present. Covers the domestic labor debate of the mid-1970's, as well as more recent works of Beechey. Stresses the importance of not treating women as a homogeneous and unitary category, and presents the shift in women's literature about women and work.

While the essays are concerned with the situation of British women, the issues raised are relevant for the research on women workers elsewhere.

185. Beechey, V. and T. Perkins. **A Matter of Hours:**
     Women, Part-time Work and the Labour Market.
     Cambridge: Polity Press, 1987.

     Updates a number of debates relating to
     women's employment, and provides evidence around
     the social construction of skill and the
     'blindness' to skills involved in the jobs women
     do. Discusses the growing significance of part-
     time jobs for their flexibility. However, the
     flexibility of part-time work is the flexibility
     desired by employers, not the flexibility desired
     by working women. The main theme is that part-time
     jobs have been constructed as such because they
     are women's jobs.
     Of great use to both academics and those
     active in the labor movement. Provides a link
     between detailed demographic studies of women's
     work and the theoretical literature.

     * *Beneria, L. (Item 18)*

186. Blossfeld, H.P.   "Labor Market Entry and the
     Sexual Segregation of Careers in the Federal
     Republic of Germany." **American Journal of**
     Sociology, 93(1) 1987, 89-118.

     Uses a large life history data base to
     describe the emergence of the basic pattern of
     sexual segregation in occupations over the life-
     course of birth cohorts and compares these
     patterns across cohorts. Discusses the importance
     of entry into the labor market for the emergence
     of sexual segregation over the life-course, and
     for the reproduction of sex-specific differences.
     Useful for the students of industrial
     sociology, sociology of occupations and women and
     work.

     * *Brewer, R.M. (Item 134)*

187. Briskin, L. and L. Yanz (eds.).   **Union Sisters:**
     Women in the Labour Movement. Toronto: The
     Women's Press, 1983.

Deals with different aspects of women's concerns in the Canadian labor movement: the historical and statistical background of women in the work force and in trade unions in Canada; specific union issues; the problem of non-unionized working women; women's experience in the union; the alliance between the labor movement and other organizations, and provides a resource section on women and unions.

Accomplishes its purpose of providing valuable documentation of the experiences of trade union women, and provides very practical information on improving the position of women in the trade union movement.

188. Bystydzienski, J.M. "Women and Socialism: A Comparative Study of Women in Poland and the USSR." **Signs**, 14(3) 1989, 668-684.

Research conducted in socialist societies emphasizes the extent to which women's circumstances in these countries are alike. This article challenges this point of view, and attempts to bring out the differences between Polish and Soviet women. The survey shows a marked difference in their views and attitudes along with their participation in the wider society of Poland and the USSR.

Well researched, this article is full of detailed information and challenges the generalization made by social science literature regarding women.

(A rejoinder to Item 212)

* Cockburn, C. (Item 235)

189. Cohen, S. **The Process of Occupational Sex Typing: The Feminization of Clerical Labor in Great Britain.** Philadelphia: Temple University Press, 1985.

Critically examines the existing theories of occupational sex-typing. Also, in explaining the feminization of clerical labor, stresses the role

of male-dominated trade unions, the process of de-
skilling and the supposed lower militancy of women
workers.
 Provides a wealth of information on the labor
force composition and changes in recruitment, and
its consequences.

(A rejoinder to Item 209)

190. Committee for Asian Women. **Industrial Women
  Workers**. Special Issue of ISIS International,
  September, No. 4, 1985.

 Discusses the common problems shared by
working women, and looks at their working
conditions in export-oriented industries as well
as newly industrialized countries in Asia. Brings
out the variations in women's work experiences and
provides shocking examples of oppressive work
relations in some cases. While providing stark
examples of assault on these workers, also
documents women's struggle, consciousness and
resistance.
 Of particular relevance to understanding
working conditions in Third World countries.

191. Cook, A.H. and H. Hayashi. **Working Women in
  Japan: Discrimination, Resistance, and
  Reform**. Ithaca: New York State School of
  Industrial and Labour Relations, Cornell
  University, 1980.

 Focuses on the little-documented lack of
equality for women in the Japanese labor market,
and looks at the ways legal, social and economic
systems affect their subordinate position.
Presents cases of women's protests and
investigates what lies ahead.
 A must for understanding working conditions
and industrialization in Japan.

192. Coyle, A. **Redundant Women**. London: The Women's
  Press Ltd., 1984.

Provides an account of the experience of redundancy by women workers in a clothing factory in Yorkshire, and discusses how structural changes facing the clothing factory are causing job loss. Evaluates the impact of closure on a predominantly female labor force, their response to job loss, and their subsequent position in the labor market. Focuses on the problems facing women, both unemployed and employed, and the nature of women's working lives.

Of particular interest to anyone interested in women's work.

193. Edwards, L. N. "Equal Employment Opportunity in Japan." **Industrial and Labour Relations Review**, 41(2) 1988, 240-250.

Examines the impact of the Japanese Equal Employment Opportunity Law on the economic position of women. Concludes that this law will not have much impact on women's position in the labor market, because of the pattern of current personnel practices of private firms and the existence of a large female labor supply.

An essential reading for understanding the Japanese labor market.

(A rejoinder to Item 107)

194. Eisenstein, S. **Give Us Bread but Give Us Roses: Working Women's Consciousness in the United States 1890 to the First World War**. London: Routledge and Kegan Paul, 1983.

Explores the formation of consciousness among wage-earning women in a period of industrialization, as well as the expansion of women's employment in the United States. Examines the tension between the late Victorian, middle class ideal of womanhood, and the actual experience of working class women. Puts the relationship between women's changing position in industry, class and family cultures, at the center of its analysis. Also brings out the complexity of women's responses to their changing position.

An excellent addition to the study of work,
women and the economy. A classic of its kind.

195. Epstein, C.F. and R. Laub Coser. **Access to Power:
      Cross-National Studies of Women and Elites,**
      London: George Allen and Unwin, 1981.

      A cross-national study of problems that women
face in pursuing high-level careers. It provides
a rigorous examination of women's access to elite
decision-making careers in the public and economic
sectors, and the professions, in the United States
and European countries, Britain, France, West
Germany, Austria, Norway, Finland, Yugoslavia, and
Poland. This series of studies demonstrate the
power of ideology in the creation of women's
positions.
      Of interest to a wide range of readership
among social scientists and the business
community.

(A rejoinder to Items 208, 214, 224)

196. Fox, B.J. and J. Fox. "Occupational Gender
      Segregation in the Canadian Labour Force,
      1931-1981." **Canadian Review of Sociology and
      Anthropology,** 24(3) 1987, 374-397.

      Gender segregation in the paid labor market
profoundly affects the working lives of women and
men. The Canadian Census of Occupational
categories shows that the decades of the 1960's
and 70's experienced decreases in gender
segregation. This discussion stresses the
shortcomings of occupational data and emphasizes
the need for a more accurate assessment of the
extent of gender segregation in paid work.
      A well-argued and thorough review of American
and Canadian literature.

(A rejoinder to Item 183)

197. Gannage, C. **Double Day, Double Bind: Women
       Garment Workers**, Toronto: Women's Press,
       1986.

       Examines the labor process in a small garment
    factory where the craft tradition persists, and
    explores in detail how craft work has been shaped
    by gender and the ethnic division of labor.
    Criticizes recent studies of the labor process as
    being sex-blind. Also combines testimonies of
    workers' experiences with a theoretical analysis.
       Important for its contribution to debates on
    class, ethnicity and gender.

    (A rejoinder to Items 149, 229)

198. Garabaghi, N.K. "A New Approach to Women's
       Participation in the Economy." **International
       Social Science Journal**, 35(98) 1983, 659-682.

       Criticizes very adequately the official
    statistics for concealing women's real
    contribution to economic life, and discusses the
    multiple-complex contribution of women to the
    economy.
       A fascinating addition to the study of
    women's role in society.

199. Grame, A. and R. Pringle. **Gender At Work.** London:
       Pluto Press, 1984.

       Adopts a comparative approach in its
    investigation of the formation of gender
    identities on the job. Examines the contradictory
    nature of the construction of gender, and shows
    how gender may take on symbolic forms in work
    places and how different aspects of work have
    gender-specific labels. Makes the important point
    that automation of the labor process has the
    potential of disrupting male domination.
       Stimulating, with important implications for
    feminist theory. For those interested in
    understanding the nature of the labor process.

200. Hacker, S.L.   "Gender and Technology at the
         Mondragon System of Producer Co-operatives."
         Economic and Industrial Democracy, 9(2) 1988,
         225-243.

         Examines the links between the issue of
     gender and organization of technology by looking
     at Mondragon, which is known as a system of
     democratically structured producer co-operatives.
     Stresses that the economic success of Mondragon
     co-operatives rests on women's unpaid labor at
     home. Men control decisions about technology.
     Gender stratification is built into manufacturing
     technology and reflects the administrative
     structure.
         Of particular relevance for students of
     technology and gender stratification.

201. Hanawalt, B.A.   **Women and Work in Preindustrial
         Europe**. Bloomington: Indiana University
         Press, 1986.

         Attempts to understand the nature of women's
     work in pre-industrial Europe.. Working women came
     from various positions in life--ranging from
     slaves, servants, and widows to professional
     midwives. The questions raised in this book have
     broad implications for understanding current
     debates on women's history.
         A scholarly work, rich in information. Makes
     a solid contribution to the study of women, work
     and society.

202. Herbenar Bossen, L.   **The Redivision of Labor:
         Women and Economic Choice in Four Guatemalan
         Communities**. Albany: State University of New
         York Press, 1984.

         Examines ways in which economic and social
     relations between sexes are redefined in
     Guatemala, combining field work with national data
     to show the sexual division of labor among the
     peasantry, the plantation workers, the middle
     class and the urban poor. Shows how economic

change alters women's status in relation to men's, and brings to bear the importance of cultural, class and regional differences.

Rich in data, this book adds to the literature on sexual stratification.

203. Humphrey, J. **Gender and Work in the Third World: Sexual Division in Brazilian Industry.** London: Tavistock Publications, 1987.

Rejects the hypothesis that women workers are 'marginalized' and confined to 'female' industries or are a 'reserve army' within the labor market. The incorporation of women into the paid labor force during the 1960's and 70's was more pervasive than previously supposed. Although women are not 'marginalized', they are prevented from occupying a prestigious position in the labor market.

Provides detailed information on the Brazilian labor market. The evidence is powerful and useful for our understanding of the organization of work in the Third World.

(A rejoinder to Item 179)

204. Jones, J. **Labor of Love, Labor of Sorrow: Black Women, Work, and the Family from Slavery to the Present.** New York: Basic Books, 1985.

Surveys black women's labor inside and outside the home, comparing it to that of their white counterparts. Analyses how their labor has affected their families, their roles in their communities, and their relations with black men. The history of black women's wage-labor is largely a history of agricultural work, domestic labor and industrial labor of the most marginal, low, dirty and worst paid variety.

An important contribution to women's history. It clarifies why generalizations about the nature of women's oppression must be made carefully, and always take into account matters of race and class.

205. Kapp Howe, L. **Pink Collar Workers: Inside the World of Women's Work**, New York: Avon Books, 1977.

       Describes, in simple language, the kinds of jobs most women hold. Women provide essential services and work as beauticians, sales workers, waitresses, office workers and homemakers. However, they are treated badly. Herein we learn about the dark side of pink-collar work.
       A journey through the economic unknown, and an addition to the literature on women, work and the economy.

(A rejoinder to Item 183)

206. Kome, P. **Somebody Has to Do It: Whose Work is Housework**. Toronto: McClelland and Stewart, 1982.

       Shows that, on the one hand , women work very hard, sometimes in a never ending daily work cycle, mothering and house caring. However, on the other hand, they are not paid for their work, it is undone quickly and so does not look as though it ever existed in the first place.
       Popularizes academic literature on this theme, and helps to understand the nature of women's work at home.

* *Kraft, J.F. (Item 247)*

207. Leacock, E., H.I. Safa and contributors. **Women's Work: Development and Division of Labor by Gender**. Massachusetts: Bergin and Garvey Publishers, Inc., 1986.

       Deals with the issue of gender inequality both at the level of household and society. Makes the point that the productive and reproductive roles of women cannot be separated, and that the division between the domestic and public domain is artificial. Demonstrates that no strategy of change confined to one level alone can succeed in eradicating female subordination, even under socialism.

Thought provoking tool for courses on women's studies, women's work and economic development.

208. Lorber, J. **Women Physicians, Careers, Status and Power**. London: Tavistock Publications, 1984.

Shows that the combination of family responsibilities and career commitments have a central place in professional women's lives. Women physicians seem to manage a demanding professional job, together with running their own households. As a result, professional socializing and informal contacts crucial to career development tend to suffer.

A thorough study of women physicians in the United States. Brings out the social mechanism of status creation for professional women.

(A rejoinder to Item 195)

209. Lowe, G.S. **Women in the Administrative Revolution**. Cambridge: Polity Press, 1987.

Analyses the changing sex composition of the office work force and discusses the causes and consequences of the feminization of clerical work. Situates this feminization in the context of the growth of large-scale organizations in industry and the public sphere. Shows that mechanization and rationalization of offices went hand in hand with a shift from male to female clerical workers.

Of particular value to students of industrial sociology, women's studies, economic and social history.

(A rejoinder to Item 189)

210. Lyson, T.A. "Industrial Transformation and Occupational Sex Differentiation: Evidence from New Zealand and the United States." **International Journal of Comparative Sociology**, 27(1-2) 1986, 53-68.

Few empirical works have examined the factors
and conditions associated with occupational sex-
segregation from a cross-cultural and a
longitudinal perspective. Lyson fills this gap,
and also examines how women's occupational
employment changed during the 1970's.
Of particular importance for its cross-
national perspective.

211. McAuley, A. **Women's Work and Wages in the Soviet
      Union.** London: George Allen and Unwin, 1981.

Looks at the high rate of female
participation in the Soviet economy and its rise
since the 1930's. Shows the existence of separate
labor markets for men and women, and how jobs in
certain sectors of the economy are 'feminized'.
On the positive side, women have been successful
in penetrating the white-collar hierarchy,
although managerial posts remain a male preserve.
An informative source which brings out the
dynamics of Soviet society and the relationship
between the state and female workers.

(A rejoinder to Items 173, 215)

212. Meier, U. "Equality without Limits? Women's Work
      in the Socialist Society of the German
      Democratic Republic." **International
      Sociology,** 4(1) 1989, 37-49.

In the German Democratic Republic, women have
a high degree of participation in the labor force.
However, there is an unequal distribution of job
opportunities for women in certain branches of the
economy. Working women face inequality of income
distribution and power relations in socialist
societies.
Despite its concentration on the German
Democratic Republic, the issues addressed here are
pertinent to the study of women and work
elsewhere.

(A rejoinder to Item 188)

* Menzies, H. (Item 251)

213. Mies, M. Patriarchy and Accumulation on a World
        Scale: Women in the International Division of
        Labour. London: Zed Books Ltd., 1987.

        Identifies the main challenges of feminism,
and claims that patriarchy and accumulation on a
world scale constitute the structural and
ideological framework within which women's reality
today has to be understood. Looks at the social
origin of the sexual division of labor, questions
socialist countries' ability to liberate women,
and calls for the development of a feminist
perspective for future society.
        Its strength lies in its ability to locate
the question of women and work within an
international context.

* Moore, T.S. (Item 355)

214. Moss Kanter, R. Men and Women of the Corporation.
        New York: Basic Books, 1977.

        Deals with the inferior status of women in
high status professional jobs, and exposes the
ultra-conservatism existent at the management
level, which dictates everything from attitude to
dress code. Views the corporate structure as too
rigid to accommodate the extensive degree of
change needed to achieve equality for women.
        Of particular interest to the students of
stratification, women and work.

(A rejoinder to Items 195, 208)

215. Motroshilova, N.V. "Soviet Women in the Life of
        Society: Achievement & Problems."
        International Social Science Journal, 35(98)
        1983, 733-746.

        Soviet women have a high rate of
participation in the labor market. They have

achieved equal rights to participate in various
social, political and economic activities.
However, the sexual division of labor still
predominates, and Soviet women see their role as
being very closely linked to that as wives and
mothers.

Despite its concentration on the Soviet
Union, this discussion raises issues that are
relevant for understanding women's position in the
labor market elsewhere.

(A rejoinder to Item 211)

216. Nicholson, N. and M.A. West. **Managerial Job
     Change: Men and Women in Transition.**
     Cambridge: Cambridge University Press, 1988.

Refutes the stereotyped notion that managers
are authoritarian guardians of power, work
obsessed and materialist in their style of values.
Discusses an interesting set of findings relating
to the experiences of male and female managers.

A welcome addition to the expanding
literature on managers, and a must for
understanding the position of women managers.

217. Okpala, A.O. "Female Employment and Family Size
     Among Urban Nigerian Women." **The Journal of
     Developing Areas**, 23(3) 1989, 439-456.

Discusses work performed by Nigerian women in
three sectors: women employed in the government
sector, those who are self-employed, and
housewives. Sheds light on the relationship
between family size and paid work.

Of importance for understanding recent
changes in the participation of women in the labor
market in Africa.

218. Pearce, D.M. "Toil and Trouble: Women Workers and
     Unemployment Compensation." **Signs**, 10(31)
     1985, 439-459.

Shows that unemployment compensation mainly goes to the relatively privileged workers--male bread-winners with 'regular' work patterns. Those who have a disadvantaged position in the labor market--i.e. women and minorities--are pushed in to a worse position by U.I. Inadequate protection against the loss of income through unemployment makes women workers, as a class, much more vulnerable to employer exploitation.

Brings out the existing inequality in the labor market, and shows how U.I. intensifies the disadvantaged position of women.

219. Penney, J. **Hard Earned Wages: Women Fighting** for **Better Work**. Toronto: The Women's Press, 1983.

Addresses themes stemming from women's experiences in the paid labor force: the struggle to get a job; female job ghettos; the challenge to get non-traditional jobs; and relations with bosses, employers, co-workers, the government, unions and one's own family. Discusses women's struggle with poverty, racism, sexual harassment and the double workday.

Of value to a broad audience. Could be used as an educational tool for teaching women to improve their situation.

* *Rogers, E.M. (Item 253)*
* *Rosen, E.I. (Item 239)*

220. Rosenfeld, R. **Farm Women: Work, Farm and Family in the United States**. Chapel Hill: University of North Carolina Press, 1985.

Documents women's contribution to farm production. Analyses the variation in farm women's work, showing that it changes according to the characteristics of the farm, the women's age and education and the age and number of children in the family. Makes it clear that women perform a wider range of tasks than is generally acknowledged.

Fills a major gap in our knowledge of the work of contemporary farm women in industrialized countries.

(A rejoinder to Items 153, 157)

221. Sachs, C.E. **The Invisible Farmers: Women in Agricultural Production**. New Jersey: Rowman and Allanheld, 1983.

Provides an account of the changing historical and international nature of farm women's involvement in agriculture; describes the evolution of domesticity as an isolated sphere for women's work; looks at the influence of capitalism on the development of the patriarchal farm family. Suggests that the combined effects of a patriarchal social system, patriarchal work arrangements, and the development of capitalism have made women's role in agriculture increasingly marginal.
A valuable addition to the scant literature on women in farming.

222. Schreiber, C.T. **Changing Places: Men and Women in Transitional Occupations**. Cambridge: MIT Press, 1979.

Rejects the hypothesis that those in sex-atypical jobs are in a position of stress because of their differences from other members of their work group, and shows that there is a general acceptance of the sex-atypical workers by supervisors, workers and co-workers.
Particularly useful for understanding the personal and organizational consequences of breaking the barriers to equality in the occupational structures.

223. Silvera, M. **Silenced: Talks with Working Class West Indian Women about their Lives and Struggles as Domestic Workers in Canada**. Toronto: Williams Wallace Publishers Inc., 1983.

Discusses some of the forces which keep immigrant women silent and prevent them from having a full speaking voice. Attempts to uncover the everyday and mundane aspects of their exploitation in the wealthy households of Toronto and supplies us with material to address the topic of women and work in the patriarchal and racist organization of the Canadian state, as shown in its immigration and labor policy.

Discusses the situation of black Caribbean domestic workers in Toronto, but this discussion is applicable to understanding the situation of domestic workers elsewhere. Broadens the basis of feminist theorization.

224. Sutton, C.D., and K.K. Moore. "Probing Opinions: Executive Women 20 Years Later." **Harvard Business Review**, 63(5) 1985, 42.

Reports the findings of a survey on the attitudes about women in business. Examines how executives view women's managerial characteristics and opportunities for advancement, and explores what these attitudes might mean for women's careers in United States' corporations today.

Important for grasping the changing nature of women's position in the labor market.

(A rejoinder to Item 195)

225. Terrell, K. "An Analysis of the Wage Structure in Guatemala City." **The Journal of Developing Areas**, 23(3) (April 1989), 405-424.

Examines individual workers' income differences by occupation, industry and personal characteristics, and looks at the importance of various forces in determining earnings. Places a major emphasis on the issue of gender related wage discrimination, and differences in the level of wages in the formal and informal sectors of the economy.

A valuable contribution to the literature on the division of labor in developing countries.

226. Valli, L. **Becoming Clerical Workers.** London:
     Routledge and Kegan Paul, 1986.

     Uses theoretical debates from the sociology
of work and education to illustrate the degree to
which social relations define the role and status
of different categories of office workers. Shows
clearly how social relations mediate and disguise
relations of power and production and provides
overwhelming evidence for the thesis that
vocational training of the sort described in this
case study reinforces gender and class
inequalities.
     Of particular use to those interested in the
role of education in reproducing occupational
structures.

227. Voydanoff, P. (ed.). **Work and Family: Changing
     Roles of Men and Women,** California: Mayfield
     Publishing Company, 1984.

     Shows how the roles of women and men in the
family are changing, and explores issues which
affect work/family relationships: unemployment,
dual career families, single-parent families, work
scheduling, day care, etc. Documents the
relevance of these issues to the lives of married
women, both at work and at home. Also examines
the institutional and individual responses to
work/family conflict, as well as the economic
difficulties among families.
     This publication is directed to undergraduate
students in the sociology of work, sex-roles,
business and management, and the sociology of
family.

228. Weiner, L.Y. **From Working Girl to Working Mother:
     The Female Labour Force in the United States,
     1820-1980.** Chapel Hill: University of North
     Carolina Press, 1985.

     Documents the extent to which women have
participated in the labor force since 1820. For
various groups of women wage-labor was at one time

controversial and debatable, but eventually became an accepted fact.

Provides a useful review of social changes precipitated by the entry of various categories of women into the paid labor force. The bibliography on the history of the government relating to this issue is particularly valuable.

229. West, J. (ed.). **Work, Women and the Labour Market**. London: Routledge and Kegan Paul, 1982.

Provides a detailed account of: the exploitation of women in the clothing industry; the sexual division of labor in electronics, and footwear factories; the reasons women's and men's careers in clerical areas of local government diverge; the reduction in women's office jobs; the difficulties immigrant women face; the problems faced by working mothers; and the history of women in the unions.

Rich in detail, highlights forces that restrict women's position in paid work.

(A rejoinder to Items 149, 197)

230. Westsood, S. **All Day, Every Day: The Factory and the Family in the Making of Women's Lives**. Urbana: University of Illinois Press, 1984.

Challenges economistic analyses of women's oppression. Rejects the dualistic approach that posits a 'gender' model for women and a 'job' model for men, and shows that gender is actively reconstructed as part of the work process. Wage-work is as much about becoming a woman as it is about becoming a worker. The performance of rituals and appropriation of popular cultural symbols make up the daily process of the construction of gender.

An extremely good study, especially in its treatment of race and ethnic differences in the formulation of gender identities.

CHAPTER THREE

THE NEW TECHNOLOGY AT WORK

.

CHAPTER FIVE

The New Technology at Work

231. Anderson, J. "How Technology Brings Blind People
     into the Work-place." **Harvard Business
     Review**, 67(2) 1989, 36.

     Advances in technology have been a boon for
people with vision loss, and have resulted in a
virtual explosion of opportunities for independent
reading and writing to visually impaired people.
Despite these improvements, visually impaired
people cannot find work suited to their interests
and skills. The main obstacle to their being
hired seems to be the discomfort most co-workers
and superiors feel in their presence.
     An illuminating account of the power of
technology and work place psychology.

232. Baxter, V. "The Process of Change in Public
     Organizations." **The Sociological Quarterly**,
     30(2) 1989, 282-304.

     Uses information from a case study on the
structural reorganization and automation of mail
processing in the United States postal service,
and investigates the extent of the changes in
technology and the authority structure in this
organization. Corporate rationality required
changes in technology and work organization, with
the intention to reduce the power of the workers.
Despite these changes, political and institutional
factors have limited improvements in productivity
and overall mail service.
     Addresses pertinent questions relating to
technology and organization of work.

233. Benson, I. and J. Lloyd. **New Technology and
     Industrial Change: The Impact of the
     Scientific Technical Revolution on Labour and
     Industry.** New York: Nichols, 1983.

     Assesses the impact of the new
microelectronic technology upon the labor

movement, and suggests policy initiatives the
labor movement might adopt as a response.
Suggests that the new technology will displace
labor and it will affect the structure of
industry. This technology has given a powerful
boost to the growth of transnational corporations,
and heightened the problems these companies raise
for the nation state. Offers an extensive
discussion of government policy toward industry
and employment during the last decade in Britain
and sees a need for changing policies appropriate
to the new environment of the electronic
revolution.
    While the focus is on Great Britain, many of
the points made are equally relevant to other
advanced industrialized countries.

* Bessant, J. (Item 19)

234. Boyle, C., P. Wheale and B. Sturgess. **People,
      Science and Technology: A Guide to Advanced
      Industrial Society.** Brighton: Wheatsheaf
      Books, 1984.

      Aims to provide an introductory account of
the ways in which science, technology and society
interrelate. It discusses the social implications
of advances in scientific knowledge, and advances
of technical innovations.
    Although it is written for science and
engineering students, it should be useful to
students of social studies, as well as the general
reader.

235. Cockburn, C. **Brothers: Male Dominance and
      Technology Change.** Pluto Press, 1983.

      Shows that the composing rooms of most
British newspapers have been transformed since
1970. Technological change has affected the task
of compositors, their labor market position and
their work environment. Explores the process of
change and the compositors' reaction to it. Shows
how employers, unions and technology mould
workers' beliefs, and indicates how composing

almost became a female occupation in the late 19th century, before male reassertion of control.
   A valuable source which brings out the ambiguities of the concept of skill and the limitations of simple 'de-skilling' theories of technological change.

236. Conference of Socialist Economists Microelectronics Group. **Microelectronics: Capitalist Technology and the Working Class.** London: CSE Books, 1980.

   Explains how the managerial introduction of microelectronics has affected labor arrangements in various sectors of the British economy. Provides a theoretical overview of, and comparative data about, the technical and social functions of microelectronics in the work place. Reveals that microelectronic production work is one of the lowest paid industrial jobs around the world, and hazards such as exposure to toxic fumes, chemical spills, and eye damage from microscopic work on chips are not uncommon. Concludes that computers are bought and used in the interest of capital. Proposes that the most effective safety method for workers is to demand a voice to negotiate with system designers about the objectives of any system before it is introduced.
   Covers many sectors, and provides valuable comparative data illustrating the range of applicability of microelectronics.

   * Cornish, M. (Item 336)

237. De. Vos, D. **Governments and Microelectronics.** Ottawa: Science Council of Canada, 1983.

   Industrial nations are looking to new technologies to maintain their competitive position in the market. From a Canadian point of view, the opportunities and threats of this new technology are compounded by the fact that other countries, like the U.S. and Japan, have a considerable head start. Draws on the experience of five countries in Europe and Scandinavia: U.K.,

France, West Germany, Sweden, and the Netherlands.
Presents brief case studies of the approach taken
by these countries and outlines the scope and
character of the initiatives being taken.
    Provides an in-depth and much needed analysis
of some of the problems and choices facing policy
makers.

(A rejoinder to Item 99)

238. Ebel, K.H. and E. Ulrich. "Some Work-place
        Effects of CAD and CAM." **International
        Labour Review**, 126(3) 1987, 351-370.

    Examines the impact of computer aided design
(CAD) and computer aided manufacturing (CAM) on
employment, organization of work, working
conditions, job content, training and industrial
relations in several countries. Shows that the
integration of CAD and CAM will be carried further
through the networking of high-speed work-
stations. The aim is paperless information
transfer from design to matching and assembly and
the culmination will be fully computer integrated
manufactuing (CIM). Suggests that only a
qualified and motivated work place can implement
this new technology. Finds little evidence of
negative employment effects.
    Brings optimism to the discussion on the
social impact of information technology.

239. Forester, T. (ed.) **The Microelectronic
        Revolution: The Complete Guide to the New
        Technology and its Impact on Society.**
        Oxford: Blackwell, 1980.

    Includes articles on the technology of the
microprocessor and its social implications, from
both sides of the Atlantic. Discusses the origin
and nature of microelectronics, the
characteristics of the microchip industry and the
increasing use of chips in every product. Details
the likely impact of this new technology on the
factory floor, the office and society. Draws
attention to the problems of a microelectronic

age. The chip is here to stay, and we must give
serious thought to our microelectronic future.
A provocative and informative source, with a
guide for further reading at the end of each
chapter.

240. Gill, C. **Work, Unemployment and the New
Technology**. Cambridge: Polity Press, 1985.

Information technology is not just another
technology and it has impact on a broad range of
activities. Examines the general impact on
companies; the automated office; effects on the
shop floor; the threat of unemployment; the
response of trade unions; the approach to new
technology adopted in Scandinavia; and overall
effects on the future of work. The new technology
poses a real threat of widespread unemployment,
and the problems involved without a massive
investment and fundamental shift in attitudes, in
organization of work and in the pattern of work
activities. Predicts the possibility of the
creation of a few creative occupations at the top,
while the rest end up with fewer skills.
Constitutes an important contribution to the
ongoing debate on the likely impact of new
technology.

(A rejoinder to Item 99)

* *Grame, A. (Item 199)*

241. Grootings, P. (ed.). **Technology and Work: East-
West Comparison**. London: Croom Helm, 1986.

Discusses the importance and difficulties of
international collaborative research in the social
sciences. Focuses on the comparative study of
work and technology between Western and Eastern
bloc countries. Provides a thorough introduction
to the sociology of work and technology in Western
Europe and the 'socialist' countries. There are
important discussions on the problem of
technological determinism and the need for

consideration of social, political and cultural
factors in the study of work and technology.
    Of interest to a comparatively specialized
academic audience.

* *Hacker, S.L. (Item 200)*

242. Heertje, A. **Economics and Technical Change.**
        London: Weidenfeld and Nicolson, 1977.

        Deals with those aspects of technology and
technical change which have dominated economic
literature from the 18th century up to the
present, showing that technological change has
profound effects on employment, power relations
and economic growth. Draws the attention of
readers to the fact that technical change can be
influenced and directed, and recommends, where
possible, democratic management of technology by
government policy.
    A valuable addition to the literature on
technology, its history and social impact.

243. Hirschhorn, L. **Beyond Mechanization: Work and
        Technology in a Post-industrial Age.**
        Cambridge: MIT Press, 1984.

        Outlines the developments which led to the
emergence of 'Cybernetic Technology', flexible
systems that are automatically controlled. This
technology will take us into the "post-industrial
age" and will have profound effects on the work
place such that workers will demand skills
completely different from those found in
conventional assembly line organizations.
Cybernetic technology will not be infallible and
workers' intervention is required to ensure system
continuity. In factories of the future, workers
are to be paid salaries rather than wages; they
are to work in teams, rotate work assignments,
train one another, and evaluate each other for pay
increases.
    Thought-provoking and highly critical of the
'de-skilling' thesis. Offers an optimistic view

of technology's impact on work and work
organization.

(Rebutted by Item 38)

244. Jaikumar, R. "Post-industrial Manufacturing."
     Harvard Business Review, 64(6) 1986, 69.

     Discusses how flexible automation is
dramatically changing manufacturing's competitive
landscape. Criticizes the managers in the United
States for using this technology poorly and not
being able to narrow the competitive gap with
Japan. As the technology installed in the United
States, lacks flexibility.
     Provides a review of the state of the art in
flexible technology and the challenges facing the
new management.

     * Kaplinsky, R. (Item 24)
     * Kaplinsky, R. (Item 99)

245. Katz, J.M. (ed.). **Technology Generation in Latin
     American Manufacturing Industries: Theory and
     Case Studies Concerning its Nature, Magnitude
     and Consequences.** London: Macmillan, 1987.

     Attempts to locate the case studies within a
theoretical context. The devotion to case studies
at the firm, industry and microeconomic levels
present a solid body of empirical data on
technological change. Based upon the conclusions
of the case studies, draws attention to the
particular problems of Latin American
industrialization, such as foreign exchange
constraints, skill availability, and so on, which
limit wider generalizability to other less
developed countries.
     A rich and fascinating book. Of particular
interest to those concerned with the issue of
technological change at the firm and industry
level.

246. Kiesler, S. "The Hidden Message in Computer
         Network." **Harvard Business Review**, 64(1)
         1986, 46.

         Discusses the impacts of technology.
    Computers are not merely a tool, but have social
    effects that can be important in the long run.
    Computers break down hierarchy and cut across
    norms and organizational boundaries. Warns
    managers to be cautious when designing systems,
    and to see in them the potential for gaining
    social benefits.
         An important discussion on the social impact
    of computers and the lessons for managers.

247. Kraft, J.F. and J.K. Siegenthaler. "Office
         Automation, Gender, and Change: An Analysis
         of the Management Literature." **Science and
         Technology and Human Values**, 14(2) 1989, 195-
         212.

         Concerns women who do information work and
    the way the computer has affected them. Compares
    general social science literature with management
    and business periodicals. Concludes that, with
    respect to employment effects and shifts in work,
    these two bodies of research assess the impact of
    microcomputers on information work very similarly.
    However, regarding issues related to labor process
    and training, the social science and management
    literature diverge a great deal. Each discipline
    has its own focus of research, but if combined,
    they yield a better understanding of the changes
    brought about by new information technology.
         An important addition to the literature on
    the social impact of technology.

248. Kraut, R.E. (ed.). **Technology and the
         Transformation of White-Collar Work.** New
         Jersey: Lawrence Erlbaum Associates,
         Publishers, 1987.

         Discusses whether computers and
    telecommunications can be introduced into the
    white-collar work place in a manner that increases

the quality of the goods and services that
organizations produce, and at the same time,
increases the quality of working life for workers.
Also provides a history of white-collar
technology, assessing its social impact, and
addresses the dynamics of designing white-collar
technology and introducing it into the office.
This work helps managers understand which
technology to adopt to bring success and
satisfaction to office life.

249. Lefebvre, L.A. and E. Lefebvre. "The Innovative
Business Firm in Canada: An Empirical Study
of CAD/CAM firms." **International Labour
Review**, 27(4) 1988, 497-513.

Compares industries with CAD/CAM technology
with other industries, regarding the impact of
computer technology on the productivity and size
of the labor force. Concludes that all categories
of employees are affected by technology; that
there is a decrease in the number of manual jobs;
that secretarial staff are most affected in the
first phase of computerization; that there is a
decrease in the number of managers; that
productivity rises, and that there is a shift from
less to more specialized jobs. These developments
could be indicative of what may take place on a
much larger scale in the next few years.
Important for understanding the social impact
of technology and the future structure of the
labor force.

250. Lynch, L.M. and P. Osterman, "Technological
Innovation and Employment in
Telecommunications," **Industrial Relations**,
28(2) 1989, 188-205.

Shows how the diffusion of technological
innovation in the telecommunications industry has
impact on employment levels. The composition of
employment in the industry has shifted toward
professional and technical employees. The
introduction of new technologies has reduced the
demand for labor in some, but has increased in

other, occupations. Technological change has
increased the functions of central offices and the
adjustment to these changes varies by union
status, gender, age, and tenure composition of
workers.
  Of significant interest to students of the
social impact of technology and the future of
work.

251. Menzies, H. **Women and the Chips: Case Studies of
     the Effects of Informatics on Employment in
     Canada.** Montreal: The Institute for Research
     on Public Policy, 1981.

     Informatics will replace paper communications
with electronic messages and will alter the nature
of work in the information-intensive service
sector of the economy. Given the concentration of
women in service sector clerical jobs, it is this
group which will bear the brunt of automation.
Computer technology will be used to create a
corporate communications network which will
transmit, process and store information. Female
clerical employees in these industries will
experience job displacement and reduced employment
prospects.
     Delivers an alarming message of crucial
importance to academics, policy makers, and
women's groups. Promotes public understanding and
discussion of key national issues.

252. Rada, J. **The Impact of Micro-electronics: A
     Tentative Appraisal of Information
     Technology.** Geneva: International Labour
     Organization, 1980.

     Covers both the abstract features of
information technology and its practical
implications and discusses the uniqueness of the
new technologies and their technical
characteristics. Sketches the likely trends on
the basis of evidence accumulated in different
sectors and fields. Focuses on the speed of the
diffusion of the technology, the different lines
of products produced and their potential uses.

The information concerning developed countries is used to examine the possible effects of information technology on developing nations.

Helps to understand, in simple language, the power of new technology and its social impact.

(A rejoinder to Items 24, 99)

253. Rogers, E.M. and J.K. Larsen. **Silicon Valley Fever.** New York: Basic Books, 1984.

Using the case of Silicon Valley in Northern California, discusses how high-tech innovation requires a decentralized management style. The organization places an enormous amount of trust in the technical competence of employees. However, the rigidity of class division is accentuated in the computer industry, where scientific and engineering personnel are insulated from the lower organizational levels of production. In fact, the production workers in the chip factories are almost all women, often Third World women. The emerging pattern is a world whose apex is exclusively male, career-oriented and emphasizes technical achievement. At the other end is an economically insecure, largely female work force.

Provides information on the people who design and produce computers, as well as the sex and class-based hierarchy in the high-tech industry.

* Rothwell, R. (Item 115)

254. Salerno, L.M. "What Happened to the Computer Revolution?" **Harvard Business Review,** 63(6) 1985, 129.

Examines the uneven progress of the computer revolution by pointing out some of the problems that have stalled its application. Evaluates the extent to which the revolution is taking place, and discusses the problems which come with the electronic era. Points out the potential difficulties that managers ought to be aware of.

Pertinent for the issues on new technology and its impact.

255. Shallis, M. **The Silicon Idol: The Micro
       Revolution and its Social Implications.**
       Oxford University Press, 1984.

       Explores the power of the computer as icon
and metaphor in shaping cultural imagination.
Condemns technology as idolatry, an instrument
that tells us nothing about our intrinsic human
nature. Technology is seen as a centralizing
power which isolates masses. Quality is replaced
by quantity, man is abstracted from nature,
mechanization replaces human activity. Believes
that the aim of the late 20th century technology
is the complete conquest of nature and
environment.
       The pessimistic account of technology
presents some controversial issues which would be
of interest to students of social impact of
technology.

       * *Shirley, S. (Item 118)*

256. Slater, P. (ed.). **Outlines of Critique of
       Technology.** London: Humanities Press, 1980.

       Criticizes an ideology which maintains that
science and technology are 'neutral' and can be
abstracted from capitalist relations of
production. Also links studies on the philosophy
of science, the labor process, and the capitalist
mode of production.
       Presents writings which were not previously
available in English, but are important for their
critical approach.

257. Stoneman, P. **The Economic Analysis of
       Technological Change.** Oxford: Oxford
       University Press, 1983.

       Looks at technological change from an
economists's point of view, evaluating the common
belief in the economic theory that the rate and
direction of technological advance is endogenous
to the economic system. Also provides a thorough

survey of the economic literature on the diffusion
of technology, and examines the impact of the new
technology on employment, investment, income
distribution, output, and market structure.

A relevant source for undergraduate and
graduate students of economic history,
technological change, and economic development.

258. Turkle, S. **The Second Self: Computers and the
Human Spirit.** New York: Simon and Schuster,
1984.

Explores the power of the computer and the
world it creates. Investigates how ideas specific
to technical communities move out and penetrate
popular culture, carrying with them a new
vocabulary for self-description. Shows that
computers change the way people think, especially
about themselves. Speaks of a 'computational
culture', armed with new metaphors of mind as
program. This new culture holds out the hope that
the widespread computerization of society will not
mean inhuman regimentation, but endless
creativity.

A remarkable book, full of insights for
understanding the power of new technology.

259. Volti, R. **Society and Technological Change.** New
York: St. Martin's Press, 1988.

Provides a broad outline of the key
characteristics of technology, as well as a
description of the cultural and social elements
that affects the development of its application.
Examines how new technology originates and
diffuses, and looks at the connection between
technological advance and rational thought. In
doing so, the transfer of technology from one
nation to another and from one organization to
another is looked at, along with problems
encountered by poor countries when they adopt
technologies that originate in rich nations, and
the feasibility of restricting the export of
technology. Concludes with stimulating thoughts

on the issue of controlling technology through the
institutions of representative government.
    Presents perspectives, theories and facts
that help to understand the impact of
technological change. Useful for courses on
technology and society.

260. Walsh, J.P. "Technological Change and the
        Division of Labor: The Case of Retail
        Meatcutters." **Work and Occupations**, 16(2)
        1989, 165-183.

        Deals with the effects of technological
change on the division of labor and skill in the
craft occupation in a service industry.
Technological change does not solely rely on the
desire of management to control the labor process,
but also on the strength of the workers'
organization and the limitations imposed by other
factors. Technological change can lead to either
a decrease or an increase in skills, or can leave
them unchanged.
        Of particular interest to those engaged in
the debate on the impact of technology on the
labor process.

261. Watanabe, S. **Microelectronics, Automation and
        Employemt in the Automobile Industry**.
        Chichester: John Wiley and Sons, 1987.

        Focuses on case studies done in Brazil,
France, Italy, Japan, and the United States.
Assesses the employment related impact of
microelectronic technology. While concentrating
on numerically controlled machines (NC) and
robotic applications, much attention is given to
the claim that microelectronics will reduce
employment in the global automobile industry.
Concludes that large job losses cannot be
attributed to the application of new technology.
        A solid contribution to the literature on the
industry-specific employment consequences of
microelectronic innovation.

262. Wilkinson, B. **The Shopfloor Politics of New Technology**. Exeter, N.H.: Heinemann Educational Books, 1983.

Explores the effects of the new technology in four case studies. Wilkinson's primary contention is that neither the adoption of particular technologies nor the organization of work based on these technologies is objectively determined, but is the result of negotiations between managers and workers. Questions that the adoption of technical innovations is determined by the pressure of competitive survival and that technology dictates the form of work.

Offers an important insight for research on technological change. The cases are interesting, and the book is useful for policy makers and researchers.

263. Zarkopvic, M. "The Effects of Economic Growth and Technological Innovation on the Agricultural labor Force in India." **Studies in Comparative International Development**, 22(1) 1987, 103-120.

Analyses some of the effects of economic growth and technological innovation on the agricultural labor force in North India. Concludes that agricultural technology helped to determine the size of the labor force in this region. The green revolution is seen as both labor displacing and labor absorbing. In this particular case, the new technology resulted in the predominance of male workers in the agricultural sector.

The findings here have implications for the application of technology in agriculture in developing countries and their employment structure.

264. Zicklin, G. "Numerical Control Machining and the Issue of Deskilling." **Work and Occupations**, 14(3) 1987, 452-466.

Looks at the debate on the effects of numerical control (NC) machining on the skill of machinists. Finds that NC machining has clearly affected the skill mix of the machinist/operator. There is no simple answer to whether machinists have been de-skilled and, if so, to what degree.

A case study showing the complexity of the impact of technology on the skill of workers.

265. Zussman, R. **Mechanics of the Middle Class: Work and Politics Among American Engineers.** Berkeley: University of California Press, 1985.

Provides a social portrait of the engineering occupation. Shows that engineers inside the factory often stand in a position between management and labor. The key to understanding this ambivalent position is technology. Technology has led to specialization, but has not brought alienation of labor in the case of engineers. They retain a close relationship to the design of products and tools, and exercise control over the labor process. Works tends to flow in non-authoritarian ways. Thus, engineers identify more with management than with union workers.

This empirical study has important insights for our understanding of the class position of middle class occupations.

CHAPTER FOUR

WORKERS AT RISK

Unemployment and Plant Closure

266. Abrahamson, P., J. Anderson, J. Henrikson and J.
     E. Larsen. "Unemployment and Poverty in the
     Contemporary Welfare State." **Acta
     Sociologica**, 29(1) 1986, 51-60.

     Unemployment has been very high for a number
of years in the western world and it has become
increasingly difficult for policy makers to ensure
satisfactory living conditions for the long-term
unemployed. The austerity program generally
reduced the transfer of programs and resources to
the jobless. Thus, the long-term unemployed will
increasingly face poverty.
     Of interest to those concerned with the
social costs of unemployment.

267. Allen, S., A. Waton, K. Purcell and S. Wood (eds.).
     **The Experience of Unemployment, Explorations
     in Sociology 21**. London: Macmillan, 1986.

     Makes a number of important contributions:
rejects the assumption that youth unemployment is
the result of structural changes in the economy;
presents an analysis of parasuicide among
unemployed men in Edinburgh; deals with the
personal experience of unemployment; contradicts
the common belief that Asians are successful
entrepreneurs; suggests that raising the age of
those leaving school is the most significant
response to rising youth unemployment; looks at
family relations and unemployment, and emphasizes
the supportive role of the family; discusses the
fact that wives feel the additional burden when
husbands lose their employment.
     Altogether this is a mixed sample, uses a
variety of approaches and contains insight and
impressive research.

268. Ashton, D.N. **Unemployment under Capitalism: The
     Sociology of British and American Labour
     Market**. Brighton: Wheatsheaf Books, Harvester
     Press, 1986.

Attempts to evaluate the causes and
consequences of unemployment and presents a
systematic empirical comparison of the differences
in its distribution between the United States and
Britain. Shows that workers from different
segments of the labor market have divergent
unemployment experiences. While the United
States economy is better able than the British to
absorb unemployed workers, the experience of
unemployment is more devastating in the United
States.
A well researched and welcome addition to the
literature on the sociology of unemployment.

269. Bluestone, B. and B. Harrison. **The
     Deindustrialization of America: Plant
     Closings, Community Abandonment, and the
     Dismantling of Basic Industry.** New York:
     Basic Books, 1982.

Addresses the extent, causes and consequences
of deindustrialization. Documents the social and
personal costs associated with systematic and
widespread disinvestment. The profound personal
and social costs resulting from unemployment is
evaluated. Suggests that the search for more
profit has made conglomerates less willing to
honor the 'social contract' with labor as they
move in search of 'business climates.' Provides
various policy options to industrialize America.
Familiarizes the readers with the fundamental
economic problems of the 1980's and bluntly
discusses the social costs of deindustrialization.

270. Buss, T.F. and F. Redburn. **Shutdown at
     Youngstown: Public Policy for Mass
     Unemployment.** Albany: State University of New
     York Press, 1983.

Examines the impact of the closure of a large
mill factory in Youngstown on workers, their
families and communities. Looks at the workers',
policy makers', and social agencies' responses to
the plant closing. Adopts a multi-disciplinary
approach and uses the case of Youngstown to draw

conclusions about social policies appropriate to
communities in economic crisis.
   A must reading for policy makers and students
of industrial relations.

(A rejoinder to Items 269, 285)

* *Cassey, B. (Item 138)*

271. Clarke, R. **Work in Crisis: Dilemma of a Nation.**
     Edinburgh: The Saint Andrew Press, 1982.

   Evaluates the present crisis over work and
unemployment and carefully assesses the prospects
before us. Explores in-depth the significance
that paid employment has in our lives today.
Shows that unemployment is at an unacceptable
level and many are forced into a position of being
outside the paid economy semi-permanently. The
result is that we may run a two nation society.
   A must reading for anyone concerned with the
social and economic consequences of today's high
unemployment.

* *Coyle, A. (Item 192)*

272. Gerhart, P.F. **Saving Plants and Jobs.** Michigan:
     W.E. Upjohn Institute for Employment
     Research, 1987.

   Discusses why plants and jobs become
economically non-viable. Recognizes that labor
costs are only one part of the equation, and
raises a series of questions about short and long-
term factors that affect the plant closing
decision. Describes several plant closures and
reviews cases in which labor relations had either
a direct, or no explicit threat, on plant closure.
Provides some useful public and private policy
suggestions.
   A useful analysis of an important issue; can
be used as a guide for future planning. Helps in
understanding the dynamics of plant closure.

* *Gill, C. (Item 240)*

273. Ginsburg, H. **Full Employment and Public Policy:**
     The United States and Sweden. Lexington,
     Mass.: Lexington Books, D.C. Heath and Co.,
     1983.

     Contrasts the United States employment
policy with the active labor market policy of
Sweden, a country committed to full employment.
Examines various programs that constitute the
contemporary Swedish labor market policy. The real
lesson for the United States is that in the
absence of a consensus to sustain full employment,
there will be no full employment.
     Provides valuable insights, of particular
interest to policy makers and students of
comparative labor market policy.

274. Godfrey, M. **Global Unemployment: The New**
     Challenge to Economic Theory. Brighton:
     Wheatsheaf Books, 1986.

     Reviews far too broad a range of literature
on the nature and causes of unemployment and
underemployment in both developed and developing
countries, in light of recent changes in the world
economy. Attempts to summarize economic thought
on the nature and causes of unemployment in
advanced capitalist economies from the late 19th
century to the present day. Evaluates different
theories of unemployment in developing countries.
     Introduces important questions, but ideas are
not well-integrated and topics are not discussed
in-depth.

275. Goldman Leventman, P.G. **Professionals out of**
     Work. New York: The Free Press, 1981.

     Discusses unemployment among well-educated
technical workers: engineers, data analysts,
scientists, etc. Documents the social-
psychological experiences of the unemployed, and
provides unique information on temporarily
unemployed high technology workers. Reports their
feelings regarding downward mobility.

Offers valuable insights into a seldom-
studied but sociologically important issue.
(A rejoinder to Item 281)

276. Haas, G. **Plant Closure: Myths, Realities and
     Responses**. California: South End Press,
     Pamphlet # 3, 1985.

Reviews the impact of economic dislocation
and plant closure on industrial America. Provides
a broad range of examples of communities
devastated by plant shutdowns. Shows that the
exodus of American firms to low-wage countries
ultimately proves to be costly for American labor
and society. The real solution is the creation of
a system under which profit reverts to the good of
the country.
Makes a meaningful contribution to the
growing literature on plant shutdowns and
runaways.

277. Hamermesh, D.S.   "What do we Know About Worker
     Displacement in the United States?"
     Industrial Relations, 28(1) 1989, 51-59.

Worker displacement has increased in the
United States independently of the business cycle.
Wage cuts do not seem to reduce the likelihood of
displacement. Its cost is high among those
workers with greater job tenure. Minorities
suffer an above average rate of displacement,
while women and older workers are no more likely
than others to become displaced.
A valuable contribution to the sociological
analysis of displacement.

278. Hollister, R.G. Jr. and D.H. Freedman, "Special
     Employment Programmes in OECD Countries."
     International Labour Review, 127(3) 1988,
     317-334.

With the increase in unemployment in OECD
countries, Western European governments merely

became concerned with launching special programs
to reduce it. Their experience with the design,
implementation and evaluation of special
employment programs is discussed. A number of
their shortcomings brought out, and the need for
rigorous evaluation is stressed.
     Most of the considerations raised here have
great relevance for other countries.

(A rejoinder to Item 274)

279. Jonzon, B. and L.R. Wise. "Getting Young People
      to Work: An Evaluation of Swedish Youth
      Employment Policy." **International Labour
      Review**, 128(3) 1989, 337-356.

      Increasing unemployment rates among Swedish
youth during the 1970's brought intensified
government actions in the 1980's. The two
programs: 'youth opportunities' and 'youth teams'
resulted in a marked decline in the level of youth
unemployment. Some of the factors which
contributed to the successful implementation of
these programs are discussed.
     Provides important lessons for addressing
youth unemployment elsewhere.

(A rejoinder to Items 284, 293)

280. Kahn, R.L. **Work and Health.** New York: John Wiley
      and Sons, 1981.

      Provides an overview of job factors that
cause stress, pressure, overload and under-
utilization of skill, and develops a multi-
dimensional theory of job loss. Suggests that
jobs provide workers with opportunities for
productive activities and rewards which are
essential for health. Since these opportunities
can only be achieved through work, psychologically
and physically damaging effects of unemployment
can be prevented by a national policy of job
entitlement.

A highly readable, non-technical overview of the literature on unemployment and quality of work-life.

281. Kaufman, H.G. **Professionals in Search of Work: Coping with the Stress of Job Loss and Unemployment.** (Foreword by J.M. Rosow). New York: John Wiley, 1982.

Deals with job loss and finding work among professionals, who constitute a new class of vulnerable workers, and examines the psychological adjustments to joblessness over time. Provides useful information on improving employability, and looks at the barriers professionals face and what they do to find work.
Offers careful interpretations of the research on unemployment and is useful for researchers, practitioners and policy makers.

(A rejoinder to Item 275)

282. Kelvin, P. and J.E. Jarrett. **Unemployment: Its Social Psychological Effects.** Cambridge: Cambridge University Press, 1985.

Provides a social and psychological analysis of unemployment, and examines individual responses to joblessness. Explains how today's unemployed, unlike those of the 1930's, are stigmatized. Both state agencies and public opinions too frequently believe that an individual's joblessness is self-inflicted. An unemployed person's self-esteem is made highly dependent on the perception of others.
Provides insights and criticism of the social and psychological literature on unemployment. A must for those interested in the social effects of joblessness.

283. Laroque, P. "Towards a New Employment Policy." **International Labour Review**, 128(1) 1989, 1-10.

A new employment policy is needed in
industrialized societies as the rate of
unemployment increases and the working population
ages. It does not seem likely that technological
change will create enough jobs to absorb the
currently unemployed and those who are new
entrants into the labor market. A new policy is
needed to prevent inactivity of large numbers of
people in the community.
   Full of insights and suggestions for policy
makers.

284. Livingstone, I. "Unemployed Youth: Alternative
     Approaches to an African Crisis."
     International Labour Review, 128(3) 1989,
     389-407.

   Critically evaluates the youth unemployment
project and policies carried out in Africa.
Questions the diagnosis that the problem is one of
lack of employable skills. Also demonstrates
that, in most cases, special youth projects and
programs have limited coverage.
   Offers valuable suggestions for policy
purposes.

(A rejoinder to Items 279, 293)

285. Lynd, S. **The Fight Against Shutdowns:**
     Youngstown's Steel Mill Closing. New York:
     McGraw-Hill Inc., 1982.

   Discusses passionately the battle against the
shutdown of three of the largest steel mills in
Youngstown, Ohio, and shows the problems that
workers face when corporate employers decide to
close shop and move out. Also provokes the reader
to ask why the business system disregards human
costs and feelings and why unions have not been
able to stand in defence of the victims of
deindustrialization.
   An insider's view of the workers' struggle.
Of value to students of labor history, industrial
sociology, as well as workers, unionists and
managers.

(A rejoinder to Items 269, 270)

286. Mertens, L. and P.J. Richards. "Recession and
        Employment in Mexico." **International Labour
        Review**, 126(2) 1987, 229-243.

        Examines the effects of recession on
    employment in Mexico. The post-1982 depression
    has resulted in widespread poverty and
    unemployment. In contrast to 1976-77, income
    distribution has worsened because higher income
    groups have been able to benefit from the export
    of capital. The future outlook does not seem
    promising--employment opportunities will not
    increase, poorer groups will need continued income
    support and Mexico will need help from the
    international community.
        Serves as a background for understanding the
    nature of unemployment in Mexico.

    * *Pearce, D.M. (Item 218)*

287. Perrucci, C.C., P.Perrucci, D.B. Targ and H.R.
        Targ. **Plant Closings: International Contexts
        and Social Costs.** New York: de Gruyter,
        1988.

        Examines the reasons why plants close, and
    puts plant closings within the context of
    international, national and local economic
    conditions. Looks at the ripple effects of plant
    closure, which, beyond displaced workers, brings
    economic and social stress. Discusses the
    workers' response and presents a range of policy
    alternatives to deal with the problems of plant
    closure.
        Is enriched with empirical evidence, enhances
    our knowledge on the issue, and is of interest to
    researchers and students of industrial policy and
    labor studies.

288. Picot, G. and T. Wannell. **Job Loss and Labour Market Adjustment in the Canadian Economy.** Ottawa: Statistics Canada, Analytical Studies Branch, Research paper series, No. 5, 1987.

Assesses the labor market adjustment of workers who were permanently laid off between 1981-1984. Attempts to document what types of workers were most likely to experience job loss and in which industries and occupations; what happened to these workers after they lost their jobs and if they find new jobs, and how.
Provides useful information on unemployment, labor adjustment, layoffs, plant closure, and retraining.

289. Rosen, E.I. **Bitter Choices: Blue Collar Women in and out of Work.** Chicago: University of Chicago Press, 1987.

Looks at the crises working class women face upon the loss of their jobs, and the strategies they employ to deal with this. Explains very well the nature of industrial transformation and the policy response to it, the resulting changes in the female sex-typed labor market, the impact on women as shaped by their gender, ethnic and age division in the plants, and the place of wages in the family economy.
A significant contribution to our understanding of the consequences of deindustrialization in America on workers, their families and communities. An excellent study on women's work and family lives.

290. Shaw, R.P. "The Burden of Unemployment in Canada." **Canadian Public Policy,** 11(2) 1985, 143-160.

Shows that not all workers face the same risk of being unemployed. A small number of workers account for a large proportion of total unemployment in Canada and those who experience it long-term are most likely to be in the primary industry, poorly educated, with few skills and come from certain regions and ethnic groups. Identifies key target groups and provides useful suggestions for developing future programs against chronic unemployment.

Focuses on Canada, but has relevance for understanding the nature of unemployment in other industrialized countries.

(A rejoinder to Item 292)

291. Shower, B. and A. Sinfield. **The Workless State: Studies in Unemployment**. Oxford: Martin Robertson, 1981.

Provides evidence to challenge the belief that a high rate of unemployment does not involve much hardship, that the individuals unemployed are largely responsible for their condition, that the power of the union must be reduced, and that a rising rate of unemployment is unavoidable. Brings new ideas to bear on our understanding of unemployment and prepares the ground for a radically different approach. Makes it clear that a fuller social and political understanding of unemployment would help to provide better theory and better policy solutions.

An excellent source, addresses the central labor market issues of the 1980's on unemployment, illuminates our social and indeed international understanding of the phenomenon.

292. Therborn, G. **Why Some People are More Unemployed than Others**. London: Verso, 1981.

Sets out to investigate why it is that some OECD countries have managed to maintain low unemployment rates during recent years, while other countries have had soaring rates not seen since the Great Depression. Two factors are seen as crucial for understanding this rate. First, countries with low unemployment are free to independently set their own policies, and second, these countries have a national commitment to the

importance of maintaining employment for their
citizens.
   Provides several challenges for social
scientists, and raises many issues which call for
further investigation.

(A rejoinder to Item 290)

293. Wallace, C. **For Richer, for Poorer: Growing up In
      and Out of Work.** London: Tavistock, 1987.

   Focuses on what happens to those leaving
school in the context of rising youth unemployment
and changing local labor market conditions. The
discussion is organized around major aspects of
young people's lives. Concludes that a 'culture
of unemployment' in the 1980's replaced one of
youthful 'affluence' in the 1960's.
   An important study, as it seeks to capture
the transition from school to work. Arguably,
however, it excludes political beliefs and
attitudes, as well as the question of race.

(A rejoinder to Items 279, 284)

294. Zipp, J.F. "Plant Closings and Control Over the
      Work-place: A Case Study." **Work and
      Occupations,** 14(1) 1987, 62-87.

   Examines the 1980-81 relocation of GM's
Corvette plant from St.Louis to Bowling·Green,
Kentucky. Zipp interviews relocated workers,
company and union officials. Plant closing is
seen as playing an important role in the struggle
between labor and capital for control of the work
place.
   Sheds light on the social impact of plant
closings, and adds to the growing literature on
the subject.

Occupational Hazards

295. Allers, V. "Workplace Preventive Programs Cut
     Costs of Illness and Injuries." **Occupational
     Health and Safety,** 58(8) 1989, 26.

     Discusses the increasing burden of health
care costs in American industry. The simplest
solution to these rising costs is obvious--
eliminate sickness and injury. Also shows that
pre-work flexibility stretching programs have
shown positive results in holding down medical
costs, and provides a list of pre-work stretching
programs available in the United States.

296. Barth, P.S. with H.A. Hunt. **Workers'
     Compensation and Work-Related Illnesses and
     Diseases.** Cambridge: The MIT Press, 1980.

     Synthesizes much of what is known about
occupational diseases and workers' compensation,
and provides the reader with a wealth of
information on the medical, administrative, and
legal nature of the problems of compensating
occupational disease victims. Also examines the
extent of the occupational disease problem, and
brings out the difficulties associated with the
present U.S. system, which encompasses only
injuries or death incurred directly on the job or
in the work place. Stresses the difficulty
incurred by workers seeking compensation for
diseases of complicated origin involving a long
latency period as well.
     An informative and valuable study for
students and professionals in labor relations,
public health, public administration and
insurance.

     * *Benson, I. (Item 233)*

297. Berman, D.M., R.J. Carlson, J.E. Peck. **The Future
     of Work and Occupational Health and Safety
     Struggles in the United States.** New York:
     Monthly Review Press, 1978.

Shows that the issue of occupational health and safety received open debate only in the late 1960's. Up to this point, U.S. corporations responded to the concern about work accidents by setting up a business controlled compensation-safety apparatus. The unions' involvement in health and safety is also relatively recent, and although business interests have dominated governmental institutions created to regulate working conditions, increasingly workers and unions are showing concern about occupational health and safety.

The claims put forward here are supported by meticulous detail. Of value to workers, professionals, students and the public at large.

298. Bezold, C., R.J. Carlson, J.E. Peck. **The Future of Work and Health.** Dover: Auburn House Publishing Company, 1986.

Intends to identify the most important characteristic of work and the work place over the next twenty-five years in relation to health issues. Shows that, as work will change in the years ahead, so will health and health care. The key trends shaping health care will also shape the health promotion programs that will affect both workers and work places in the future. Reviews the key trends affecting work in the areas of the economy, technology, values and changes in the work place itself.

Makes the uncertainty of the future more visible, so that decisions can be made as wisely as possible.

299. Chapman Walsh, D. **Corporate Physicians: Between Medicine and Management.** New Haven: Yale University Press, 1987.

Provides an illuminating historical survey of occupational health and safety along with the emergence of the corporate physician in the United States. Comparison with the United Kingdom shows that different administrative structures of health care in the community affect how

occupational medicine is practiced. In the United
States, the CP's role has expanded to fill
capital's need for an external pressure. As in
Britain, company doctors tend to become ancillary
agents of discipline.
   Makes a valuable contribution and deserves to
be read by both medical and industrial
sociologists.

300. Chhokar, J.S. "Safety at the Work-place: A
        Behavioural Approach." **International Labour
        Review**, 126(2) 1987, 169-178.

   Critically reviews safety measures that
primarily rely on the actual incidence of
injuries. Such measures of safety have large
scale inaccuracies and contribute little towards
suggesting what can be done to prevent the
recurrence of accidents. Suggests that a
judicious combination of various approaches will
be the shortest path to the reduction of accidents
and the enhancement of safety.
   Provides new insights for improving health
and safety measures in the work place.

301. Cohen, L and C. Blackhouse. **The Secret
        Oppression: Sexual Harassment of Working
        Women**. Toronto: Macmillan, 1979.

   Focuses on seven in-depth studies which
involved interviews with a wide range of working
women and a cross section of managers, union
representatives, government officials, and
representatives of both the Canadian and American
women's movements. Sexual harassment seems to be
the rampant feature of the work place. In fact,
it is the most serious occupational hazard
confronting working women.
   Provides a range of solutions to prevent and
deal with sexual harassment.

* *Conf. of Soc. Elo. Mic. Group (Item 236)*

302. Cox, S. "Women's Work: Women's Health."
         Occupational Health, 37(11) 1985, 505.

         This discussion addresses the recent interest
     in the problems and hazards of work and their
     effects on women workers, as well as the extent
     to which women put their health and well being at
     risk. It focuses on occupations in which a large
     percentage of the employees are women, attempts to
     identify the health hazards associated with these
     occupations, and gives suggestions for improving
     their situation.

303. Crocker, K. "Cost-Effective Management of Back
         Pain." **Occupational Health**, 41(1) 1989, 24.

         Looks at a survey taken to measure the cost
     of back pain problems in one industry, showing
     that back pain costs the health service millions
     of dollars. Also provides preventive measures and
     programs to reduce the cost of back injuries.
         Another piece of evidence which stresses the
     benefits of preventive health measures for both
     employers and employees.

304. Elling, R.H. **The Struggle for Workers' Health: A
         Study of Six Industrialized Countries.**
         Farmingdale, New York: Baywood Publishing
         Company, Inc., 1986.

         The problem of work-related diseases and
     accidents is widespread and serious. Yet job
     deaths and disabilities are not equally widespread
     and as serious among countries. There are
     remarkable differences between countries in their
     protective measures. This book focuses on Sweden,
     Finland, East Germany, West Germany, the United
     Kingdom and the United States. It demonstrates
     that variations in the strengths of workers'
     movements speak strongly for the capacity of
     working people to organize for well-being.
         An excellent piece of scholarship which
     should be read by students of labor studies,
     workers and concerned managers.

305. Feingold, B.C. "Rising Costs of Substance Abuse
        Demand Effective Corporate Policies."
        Occupational Health and Safety, 58(10) 1989,
        56.

        Discusses the 'epidemic' of drug abuse in
American work places. The by-products of employee
substance abuse--lower productivity, and
escalating health care and benefit costs--are
affecting business and costing corporate America
over billions of dollars. Also provides shocking
statistics, and gives suggestions to ensure a
safer work place.

306. Folkard, S. "Shift Work- A Growing Occupational
        Hazard." **Occupational Health**, 41(7) 1989,
        182.

        The number of organizations employing some
form of shift work system is on the rise. Folkard
discusses the pros and cons of this type of work
and suggests that human beings, as a diurnal
species, are not 'designed' to work at night.
However, by applying scientific principles to the
design of shift systems, we may be able to reduce
problems by a personnel selection based on an
individual's potential for tolerating shift work.
        Of particular use to managers, workers and
unions.

307. Gersung, C. **Work Hazards and Industrial Conflict.**
        Hanover: University Press of New England,
        1981.

        Industrial hazards are seen as a basic aspect
of industrial conflict. As safety on the job is a
cost factor, employers have opted to make the
profit no matter what the cost to human life.
Notes that work hazards are less common in top
offices than on the shop floor and discusses how
these hazards, and confrontation over the cost of
compensation or prevention is part of class
conflict.

Well written and provides extensive
historical examples. Thought provoking.

308. Goerth, C.R. "Office Related Illness Increases
        Interest in Toxic-Tort Litigation."
        Occupational Health and Safety, 55(11) 1986,
        18.

        The office promises to become the newest
arena for personal injury lawyers and their
clients to square off against employers. Goerth
believes that the office work place is now
starting to catch up with what has been happening
in the industrial work place.

* *Goodman, P.S.*

309. Grayham, D.A. and V.O. Del Rosario. "OH in the
        Third World: The Background." **Occupational
        Health**, 37(8) 1985, 353.

        Despite its benefits, high technology is
presenting tremendous problems for both society
and governments in many Third World countries.
This piece discusses certain occupational health
problems which are peculiar to Third World
countries, and draws the readers attention to the
limitations of statistics, the double standards of
occupational health care services, and the
complexity of the problems in developing
economies.
        A very useful reading for anyone interested
in the issue of work in developing countries.

310. Levy, B.S. (M.D.), and D.H. Wegman (M.D.).
        **Occupational Health: Recognizing and
        Preventing Work-related Disease**. Boston:
        Little, Brown and Company, 1983.

        Discusses general concepts concerning
occupational health and its approaches to the
recognition and prevention of diseases. Describes
various types of occupational hazards and their

effects on workers, and addresses workers'
compensation and the problems faced by minorities
and women's groups. The emphasis is on the vital
role of the health professional in the prevention
of work-related injuries.
  Integrates the contributions of many
specialists from varied disciplines. This can be
used as a textbook for students, as well as a
reference for primary health care providers.

311. Makower, J. **Office Hazards: How Your Job Can Make
     You Sick**. Washington, D.C.: Tilden Press,
     1981.

  Office hazards are more subtle than most
industrial hazards. They work cumulatively--over
long periods of time, and scientists are just
beginning to identify them. Makower attempts to
bring to light the nature of office hazards, and
makes it clear that the hazards we face in offices
are not individual problems, but linked with a
particular method of work organization.
  Provides a frightening new look at office
work, and is an important guide-book for workers,
managers and union activists.

312. Navarro, V., and D.M. Berman (eds.). **Health and
     Work Under Capitalism: An International
     Perspective**. Farmingdale, New York: Baywood
     Publishing Inc., 1983.

  Essays in this volume have appeared in the
pages of the **International Journal of Health
Services** during the last few years. Critically
looks at the dominant ideology for regarding work
as unproblematic, and draws attention to the
reality of the hazard of work under capitalism.
It also discusses the subordination of workers
under capitalism. This domination has even more
harmful consequences for the health of the
laboring population in developing countries.
Brings out various dimensions of work-related
disease and injuries as well.
  A definite eye-opener for grasping the
problems in the world of work today.

313. Nelkin, D. and M.S. Brown. **Workers at Risk:**
     Voices From the Work Place. Chicago: The
     University of Chicago Press, 1984.

     Criticizes the field of occupational health
     and safety for neglecting the perceptions and
     concerns of the workers themselves. The authors
     interviewed workers who are exposed to chemical
     hazards at work, and assume that perception of
     risk, and adaptations to hazardous work, take
     place in a nexus of social, political, and
     economic conditions. They investigate how such
     conditions influence the attitude and response
     toward risk.
     This work deals with a fundamental topic and
     presents the views of the workers in their own
     language.

314. Page, J.A. and M. Win. O'Brian. **Bitter Wages.** New
     York: Grossman Publisher, 1972,

     Covers a broad spectrum of the American
     industrial scene, and gives a devastating
     analysis, providing evidence from on-the-scene
     descriptions, interviews, statistical research,
     excerpts from official hearings, etc. Also spells
     out 'the silent violence' which takes place in the
     work place and criticizes the government,
     industry, unions, workers compensation system for
     impeding any significant progress towards reducing
     the epidemic of occupational trauma and disease
     sweeping the nation.
     A thorough documentation, but a horror story
     of safety, or lack of it, on the job. Although
     the focus is on the U.S., it is relevant for all
     industrial countries.

315. Polakoff, P.L. "Satisfaction With Work is
     Strongest Factor in Predicting Longevity."
     Occupational Health and Safety, 58(4) 1989,
     37.

     Workers attach a range of meaning to their
     work. For many adults, work is the most

significant way of participating in society and
establishing an identity. This entry shows that
every job, in varying degrees carries with it
specific requirements for physical, intellectual,
psychological and social functioning. Work can
become a health giving activity, instead of a
daily grind.

316. Polakoff, P.L. **Work and Health: It's Your Life.**
     Washington, D.C.: Press Associates, Inc.,
     1984.

     Shows that job-related disease is a national
problem in the United States, and that there is a
struggle taking place every day in the work place.
The death toll from on the job accidents is about
the same as the Vietnam war. The bitter truth
about work-related hazards, and the complex
problem associated with this, is also adequately
brought out.
     Helps shop stewards, manager and working
people to be better informed and make the work
place safer.

317. Reasons, C.E., L.L. Ross, and C. Paterson.
     **Assault on the Worker: Occupational Health
     and Safety in Canada.** Toronto: Butterworths,
     1981.

     Reveals the shocking fact that Canada has one
of the worst work place safety records in the
industrialized world and documents various forms
of assault by type of hazard and type of work.
Attacks the drive for productivity and profit for
disregarding the health and safety of workers.
Also provides alternative approaches, which get
their primary impetus from the workers themselves.
     Rich in data and provides an extensive list
of literature, films and workers' organizations.

318. Reed, J.C. "Excessive Stress Affects Worker,
     Health, Productivity." **Occupational Health
     and Safety,** 53(9) 1984, 33.

Few organizations give much attention to stress on the job. The focus, instead, is on production goals, quarterly reports, and profits-- often at the expense of the worker. This article shows the devastating effects of stress on both the worker and work performance.

Provides suggestions for handling stress and minimizing its negative effects. Of value to managers, workers and unions.

319. Rosner, D. and G. Markowitz. **Dying for Work: Workers' Safety and Health in Twentieth Century America**. Bloomington: Indiana University Press, 1987.

Illuminates the interrelationship between industrial and social organizations and workers' health and looks at the alternative models that have been developed for addressing the issues of prevention of, and compensation for, industrial accidents and diseases. Addresses the development of government regulation of safety and health in the plant and examines political and scientific issues surrounding lead--the most ubiquitous industrial poison. As well, it evaluates the social and economic conditions surrounding asbestos-related disease, by sinosis, and radium poisoning.

A rich account of the characteristics of hazards associated with modern industrial society is found in this piece. A required reading for anyone interested in the issue of work.

320. Shostak, A.B. "Coping with Blue Collar Stress is Solvable Management Challenge." **Occupational Health and Safety**, 55(11) 1985, 19.

Discusses the complex sources of stress for blue-collar workers. Plant shut-downs, technological unemployment, hazardous work places, and insufficient income levels are among the many causes of stress. Shows how management, labor and the rank and file might respond in a cost-conscious, creative and effective manner.

321. Stellman, J.M. **Women's Work, Women's Health:**
     Myths and Realities. New York: Pantheon
     Books, 1977.

     Focusing on women, this book brings out the
physical and psychic strain of working on the
assembly line, in offices and hospitals, and at
home. It provides a telling reexamination of the
myths and oversights surrounding women who work,
gives vital information about work hazards, and
suggests what women can do, together and
individually, to create a safer working
environment.
     Helps to understand the totality of the work
experience. It ought to be read by physicians and
nurses who practice occupational health, workers,
researchers and policy makers.

322. Sward Rapaport, D. "Exposure to Mercury Vapor
     Endangers Workers' Mental, Physical Health."
     Occupational Health and Safety, 58(10) 1989,
     47.

     Discusses the dangers associated with mercury
poisoning and identifies the industries in which
this substance is used. Mercury vaporizes easily
at room temperature, becoming an invisible,
odorless poison. Also gives the list of
instruments that can identify the presence of
mercury.
     This discussion shows the danger of mercury
poisoning associated with certain types of work.
Of value to occupational health nurses, workers,
and unions.

323. Tramposh, A. "Musculoskeletal Injuries Demand New
     Treatment Model." **Occupational Health and**
     Safety, 58(4) 1989, 20.

     Shows that workers' compensation benefit
payments have risen sharply. The majority of
injuries were musculoskeletal in nature: injury to
virtually any body part involving muscles,
tendons, ligaments, joints, bones or peripheral

nerves. Draws attention to the complexity of the
problem, and gives advice to prevent or attack
injury as well.

324. Vakavanidis, A. and N. Sarafopoulos. "Occupational
        Health and Safety in Greece: Current Problems
        and Perspectives." **International Labour
        Review**, 128(2) 1989, 249-258.

        Deals with recent advances in occupational
health and safety in Greece and discusses existing
problems in the Greek work place. Evaluates the
Health and Safety Act of 1985 and concludes that,
despite the advances made in recent years, there
is a need for rigorous reorganization of
institutions.
        Although the focus is on Greece, the issues
raised in this discussion are relevant for other
countries.

325. Weindling, P. **The Social History of Occupational
        Health.** London: Croom Helm, 1985.

        The discussion is restricted to industrial
occupational health and aims to establish it as
part of the social history of industrialization.
Draws an international comparison, and shows how
occupational health has been affected by a complex
variety of social factors. A wide range of
excellent case studies makes the important point
that disabilities and diseases are not only the
most acute expressions of social inequality, but
also have a general effect on living conditions.
The understanding of occupational health is
inextricably related to broader socioeconomic
conditions in industry.
        Poses a challenge to historians and the
common belief regarding occupational health.

326. Willim, H. "Trade Unions and Occupational Safety
        in the German Democratic Republic."
        International Labour Review, 126(3) 1987,
        329-336.

In the German Democratic Republic trade
unions have played a major part in protecting
their members' health and safety. Occupational
safety representatives on the shop floor,
voluntary safety inspectors, enterprise safety
sub-committees, extra-enterprise safety
inspectors, and a three-tier system of daily,
weekly, and monthly supervision have all helped to
promote the existence of a safer work place.
These attempts are backed by safety training
programs for union representatives and inspectors
as well as information carried to various media.
       The information provided here could be used
as an example of how to achieve a safer work
place.

327. World Health Organization. **Early Detection of
       Occupational Diseases**. Geneva: World Health
       Organization, 1986.

       Evaluates methods for the early detection of
health impairment among employed workers and
provides a general description of categories of
health impairment. Deals with clinical laboratory
tests used to detect occupational diseases in the
body's main organs. The long and detailed
bibliography lists additional sources of specific
substances, along with research studies.
       A useful guide for occupational health
specialists, policy makers, workers and workers'
representatives.

328. Wooldandler, S. "Toxic Injury to Male Reprodctive
       System." **Occupational Health and Safety**, 52
       1983, 24.

       Reviews the relatively few occupational
studies, along with the more extensive laboratory
and therapeutic data, in the field of male
reproductive toxicity. Shows the danger of toxic
exposure, and calls for further study and an
increase in the awareness of this hazard.
       Of value to all who work. Makes it clear
that work injuries affect not only the individual
workers, but their families.

CHAPTER FIVE

THE TRADE UNIONS, INDUSTRIAL CONFLICT AND STRIKE

The Trade Unions, Industrial Conflict and Strike

329. Abella, I.M. **Nationalism, Communism and Canadian Labour**. Toronto: The University of Toronto Press, 1973.

Documents the interplay of nationalism, communism and international unionism on the development of the Canadian labor movement between 1935 and 1956. Discusses in detail the early development of each of the major industrial unions, and the struggle within and between CIO and CCL. Early industrial unions were left-wing and the product of Canadian, not American, initiatives. However, in the 1940's and 1950's, the direction of the union leaned to status quo, conciliatory unionism.
Has some shortcomings, but provides an excellent account of the history of Canadian Labor.

330. Barbash, J. "Thinking Ahead: Do we Really Want Labor on the Ropes?" **Harvard Business Review**, 63(4) 1985, 10.

Reviews current developments in industrial relations in the United States. Suggests that, in the United States, the balance of power has shifted from the unions to employers. Employers are aggressively attacking the basic organizational rights of labor and this raises disturbing questions about the social consequences of the unions' declining power.
An eye-opener and a must for understanding the challenges facing American labor today.

331. Bergquist, C. **Labor in Latin America: Comparative Essays on Chile, Argentina, Venezuela and Colombia**. Stanford: Stanford University Press, 1986.

Challenges twentieth-century Latin American historiography, and attempts to show the extent to which organized labor played a decisive role in the evolution of Latin American societies. Not only discusses the role of labor, but looks at the broad pattern of the social development of Chile, Argentina, Venezuela and Colombia. Perhaps, its major weakness is that it exaggerates the importance of export sector workers and makes little reference to state employees or white-collar workers.

An outstanding work of scholarship; full of insights for comparative purposes.

(A rejoinder to Items 341, 365)

332. Blum, A.A., M. Estey, J.W. Kuhn, W.A. Wildman, L. Troy. **White Collar Workers**. New York: Random House, 1971.

Focuses on the relationship between white-collar workers and the unions. Looks at clerical employees, engineers, retail clerks, teachers and white-collar employees in the federal government and suggests that the relationship that develops between unions and white-collar workers will help to determine the future of the American labor movement.

An important source for tracing the early studies in this area.

333. Bonnell, V. **Roots of Rebellion: Workers' Politics and Organizations in St.Petersburg and Moscow**, 1900-1914. Berkeley: University of California Press, 1983.

Attempts to answer the question of why the Russian trade unions became the vehicle for revolution rather than reform, while the reverse occurred in other parts of the world. In Russia, trade unions were concerned not only with workers' rights in the work place, but with the citizenship rights of free speech, free press and free assembly. In the process, they became identified ideologically and organizationally with the opposition parties.

A rich volume on the sociology of the trade unions and a significant contribution, both theoretically and empirically.

* *Briskin, L. (Item 187)*

334. Bronstein, A.S. "The Evolution of Labour Relations in Uruguay: Achievements and Challenges." **International Labour Review**, 128(2) 1989, 195-212.

Reviews the evolution and the system of industrial relations in Uruguay, which is unique in Latin America. This System does not have any institutional framework for the conduct of collective bargaining. With the political and economic crisis that Uruguay experienced after 1960's, the labor relations system entered a long dark period. The situation has changed since 1985, and there has been a return to a dialogue between the government, the employers and the unions.
Of value to the student of industrial relations in Third World countries.

335. Cornfield, D.B. "Plant Shutdowns and Union Decline: The United Furniture Workers of America; 1963-1981." **Work and Occupations**, 14(3) 1987, 434-451.

Addresses the effects of the changing social, political and economic environment on unions and their ability to recruit and retain members. Draws on 163 local unions of the United Furniture workers between 1963 and 1981. Suggests that the declining capacity of unions to charter large locals had a greater impact on union decline than did adverse effects of geographical capital redistribution.
Adds insight to the current discussion on declining union membership.

336. Cornish, M. and L. Ritchie. **Getting Organized: Building a Union**. Toronto: Women's Press, 1980.

Describes in detail the process of unionization and certification, starting with the need for collective action to win rights and dignity at work and ending with negotiating the first contract. Highlights the section of the law which can be used for the benefit of workers. The target groups of this book are women workers in offices and immigrant women workers in small factories and the service sector.
Provides guidance on the legal and technical aspects of organizing. Although examples are given in the context of Ontario's labor laws, workers in general would find much of the information relevant to their own situations.

337. Edlund, S. **Labour Law: Research in Twelve Countries**. Stockholm: Swedish Center for Working Life, 1986.

Discusses the development tendencies and the general status of labor law research in Denmark, Finland, Sweden, the Federal Republic of Germany, the Netherlands, Belgium, France, Italy, Britain, the United States, Canada, Australia and Yugoslavia. Outlines the major contributions in the field and the major outlets for research. The general theme is that labor law tends to be unaware of what is happening in the real world.
An important contribution to the literature on labor law, and an invaluable reference tool for readers with substantial knowledge of labor law frameworks.

338. Floor, W. **Labour Unions, Law and Conditions in Iran (1914-1941)**. Durham, U.K.: Center for Middle Eastern and Islamic Studies, University of Durham, Occasional paper series, No. 26, 1985.

Provides detailed information about the pre-1941 labor movement in Iran. Suggests that workers generally accepted their status of relative economic deprivation, that there were few committed labor leaders, and that workers exhibited docile behaviour. Unfortunately, Floor does not take Reza Shah's repressive labor policies into account and uses British diplomatic reports as his major source.

Despite shortcomings, provides a wealth of facts and is a welcome addition to the 20th century Iranian labor history.

(A rejoinder to Item 349)

339. Freeman, B. **1005: Political Life in a Union Local**. Toronto: James Lorimer and Company, 1982.

Examines democracy and oligarchy within local 1005 of the United Steel Workers of America (USWA) in Canada. Since 1946, this local has represented a large number of Steelco workers in Hamilton. These workers presented the company with a series of demands which the company refused to meet and this impass resulted in a long strike. For analysts like Freeman, the question is how could steel workers expect to win their demands in the context of an ever-growing economic recession. The answer to this question lies in understanding the historical development of local 1005.

A crucial study of the workers' struggle and problems in Canada.

340. Ginger, A.F. and C. David (eds.). **The Cold War Against Labor**. (2 vols.) Berkeley: Meiklejohn Civil Liberties Institute, 1987.

An extraordinary anthology which starts with the union-bashing of today, then describes its roots in the McCarthy era. Provides telling stories of many unions over the decades. Puts forward the thesis that there is a vital link between the struggle for the rights of American labor and the worldwide movement for peace.

Filled with facts and ideas for today and
tomorrow, and a must for understanding the issues
confronting American labor. Of particular
interest to those working in the labor movement
for peace, jobs and justice.

341. Greenfield, G.M. and S.L. Maram. **Latin American
     Labor Organizations**. Westport, Conn.:
     Greenwood Press, 1987.

Deals with the history and current state of
trade union organizations in Latin America. It
encompasses not only all the Spanish- and
Portuguese-speaking countries, including Puerto
Rico, but also Belize, French Guiana, Guyana,
Haiti, Jamaica, and Suriname--just some of a total
of 28 countries. Summarizes the evolution and
contemporary position of trade union
organizations; provides a bibliography of source
materials; and a review of important individual
labor organizations.
A major contribution; no other source
contains so large a quantity of information on the
topic; an excellent reference book.

(A rejoinder to Items 331, 365, 369)

342. Hanami, T. **Labor Relations in Japan Today**. Tokyo:
     Kodansha International Ltd., 1979.

Informs western readers that conflict exists
in Japanese industrial relations. However, it
takes a different form than in the west and cannot
be handled in the same way. Discusses the unique
character of dispute settlement in Japan and
attempts to analyze the malaise of the trade union
movement, as well as the industrial relations
system as a whole, in the light of new
developments in the post-industrial society.
A carefully researched and comprehensive
description of Japan's trade union structure,
legislation and dispute procedure.

(A rejoinder to Items 47, 66, 105, 356)

343. Jackson, M.P. **Trade Unions**. London: Longman, 1982.

    Summarizes the numerous empirical studies made on trade unions in the 1970's. Includes seven major topics: trade union growth and development; white-collar and non-manual workers' trade unionism; internal democracy; the challenge from shop floor; collective bargaining and economic objectives; trade union: conflict or compromise; trade unions and governments.
    Fills the demand for an introductory textbook on trade union studies done in the 1970's in Britain and other English-speaking countries.

344. Jacobi, O., F. Jessop, H. Kastendiek and M. Regini (eds.). **Economic Crisis, Trade Unions and the State**. London: Croom Helm, 1986.

    Deals with the general aspects of the current economic crisis and provides a thematic survey of economic performance in western Europe. The crisis of post-war capitalism may be seen to result from two shifts in economic organization-first, the impact of new technologies on mass production industries, and secondly, the current decline in the U.S. hegemony in international economic relations.
    Full of insights and poses interesting questions for future research.

    (A rejoinder to Item 346)

345. Jain, A. (ed.). **Solidarity: The Origin and Implications of Polish Trade Unions**. Baton Rouge: Oracle Press, Ltd., 1983.

    With the progress in general education, more contact with the west, and the change in Soviet style socialism, Poles are looking more and more for alternatives. The temporary establishment of an independent trade union movement provided a great support to other autonomous institutions. The underground opposition remains strong,

solidarity still survives, and its formal
suppression has even contributed to its
perpetuation.
    Of particular use to students of Polish labor
studies.

346. Kochan, T. (ed.). **Challenges and Choices Facing
         American Labor.** Cambridge: MIT Press, 1985.

    Labor leaders have found themselves in the
era of 'concession bargaining' as they struggle to
save their members' jobs from foreign and non-
union domestic competition. Are problems facing
the labor movements temporary or will they
transform industrial relations in the United
States? This is the major question that Kochan
intends to answer.
    Provides a sobering view of labor movements
and the problems they face. A must reading for
students of American labor.

(A rejoinder to Item 344)

347. Kochan, T.A., D.J.B. Mitchell, and L.Dyer (eds.).
         **Industrial Relations Research in the 1970's:
         Review and Appraisal.** Madison, Wis.:
         Industrial Research Association, 1982.

    Provides a review and evaluation of research
in the field of industrial relations over the past
decade. Covers a range of specific areas:
international and comparative industrial
relations; wage determination and public policy;
employment and training programs; organizational
behavior and industrial relations; labor history;
a critical appraisal of research on union and
collective bargaining; and appraisal of a decade's
research.
    An excellent source enriched with a long
bibliography. Deserves a wide readership.

348. Korpi, W. **The Working Class in Welfare
     Capitalism: Work, Unions and Politics in
     Sweden.** London: Routledge and Kegan Paul,
     1978.

     Analyses union politics in a welfare state
where workers have considerable political power.
Develops an elaborate theoretical framework and
concludes that the working class in advanced
capitalist societies continues to pose a challenge
to the economic system. Discusses the uniqueness
of Sweden on several important dimensions.
     An important contribution to the sociology of
work, this book provides a wealth of data.

349. Ladjevardi, H. **Labor Unions and Autocracy in
     Iran.** Syracuse: Syracuse University Press,
     1985.

     A pioneering study that seeks to answer why
an independent trade union movement failed to
develop in Iran between 1906 and 1963.
Demonstrates how powerful forces were ready to
cooperate with the government in suppressing labor
unions. Foreign governments also used their
influence against the unions. This was especially
true of Great Britain, which prior to 1953 owned
the Anglo-Iranian oil company, the largest
industrial employer in the country. The
suppression of the unions prevented workers from
participating in the political process. Thus,
they had no interest at all in preserving the
system.
     An important contribution which fills a major
gap on the history of the labor movement in Iran.

(A rejoinder to Item 338)

350. Leicht, K.T. "Unions, Plants, Jobs, and Workers:
     An Analysis of Union Satisfaction and
     Participation." **The Sociological Quarterly,**
     30(2) 1989, 331-362.

Discusses the relationship between unions and their members, and tests union satisfaction and participation in the United States' manufacturing industries. Provides qualified support for the theory which predicts that union members will be satisfied with their unions and participate more in them, if there are extensive ties between unions, employers and workers.

Relevant for understanding the internal dynamics of unions, and useful for the future of unionization and organization of work.

351. Levant, V. **Capital and Labour: Partners? Two Classes – Two Views.** Toronto: Steel Rail Educational Publishing, 1977.

Attempts to clarify the nature, characteristics and forms of company unionism, and traces its emergence and development in North America and Canada. Also aims to analyze and explain the major factors sustaining its existence.

Questions the ideological basis of the contention that labor and capital are partners.

352. Lipset, S.M. (ed.). **Unions in Transition: Entering the Second Century.** San Francisco: Institute for Contemporary Studies Press, 1986.

Provides useful reviews of various themes facing unions today: the developments in public sector unionism, the internal union democracy, and the economic impact of unions. Compares the United States with Canada, and shows that the decline of the American unions cannot be explained by the changing composition of the labor force.

Addresses crucial questions and brings out the distinctiveness of American unions.

(A rejoinder to Items 362, 377)

353. McCord, N. **Strikes.** New York: St. Martin's Press, 1980.

Examines, through the study of strikes between 1790 and 1970, the changing nature of industrial disputes in Britain and the United States. Looks at a number of specific strikes as historical events, and tries to bring out the complexity of the historical context in which they occurred. Also makes the important point that it is difficult, perhaps impossible, to establish a convincing common core of explanation for these disputes.

Gives students of history a number of examples of industrial disputes, together with suggestions of sources for more extended study.

354. McDermott, J. **The Crisis in the Working Class and Some Arguments for a New Labour Movement,** Boston: South End Press, 1980.

Provides a historical account of the labor movement in the United States and criticizes trade unionism as practiced in the U.S. today. Presents penetrating views of the working class and suggests radical changes for workers and their organizations.

Creative, provocative and written as a guide to a strategy for radical change.

355. Moore, T.S. "Are Women Workers 'Hard to Organize'?" **Work and Occupations,** 13(1) 1986, 97-111.

It cannot be assumed that women are less interested than men in union membership. On the contrary, this representative national survey of the United States reveals that unorganized women workers are more likely to desire union representation than their male counterparts.

Serves as a cautionary note to analysts not to attribute differences in organizational membership to attitudes that have never been demonstrated.

* *Morehouse, W. (Item 27)*

356. Ohta, T.   "Work Rules in Japan." **International Labour Review,** 127(5) 1988, 627-639.

     Analyses the relevant legislative provisions and work rules in Japan and their place in labor management relations. The labor management consultation system has developed considerably in recent years in large enterprises. However, in small and medium-sized firms the situation is different and the unionization rate has dropped. This means that over two-thirds of Japanese workers are not organized.
     Provides an insider's view of work rules in Japan.

     (A rejoinder to Items 47, 66, 105, 342, 369)

357. Ozaki, M. et al.   **Labour Relations in the Public Service: Developing Countries.** Geneva: International Labour Office, 1988.

     Contrasts public service labor relations between developing countries and the industrialized market economy. Shows clearly the difference between the two groups of countries and emphasizes the limitations of the trade union rights in the developing countries. Provides detailed comparative studies of the following countries: Algeria, India, Malaysia, Peru, the United Republic of Tanzania and Venezuela.
     Of particular interest to those concerned with the labor relation issues in the growing sector of employment in the developing world.

358. Ozaki, M.   "Labour Relations in the Public Service." **International Labour Review,** 126(4) 1987, 405-422.

     Examines labor disputes and disagreement between the public servants' union and public employers, arising out of the determination of employment conditions or other labor relations issues. Brings out the dual nature of government

in relation to the public sector and the problems
that the public sector unions face today.
    Relevant for understanding the role of the
state in restricting the scope of labor relations.

(A rejoinder to Item 375)

359. Panitch, L. **Working Class Politics in Crises.**
        London: Verso, 1986.

        Considers the nature of the decline of the
union's power and the future of working class
politics. The ideology and practice of social
democratic parties, i.e. the British labour party,
have contributed to a decline in class politics
and working class identity. As well, the neo-
corporatist political and economic structures of
the post-World War II period were intended to
accommodate the trade union movement to the
functions of accumulation and legitimation of the
capitalist state
    Makes a fine integrated case regarding the
dangers of social democracy and neo-corporatism
for the advancement of the working class.

* *Phizacklea, A. (Item 170)*
* *Piore, M.J. (Item 31)*

360. Poole, M. **Theories of Trade Unionism : A
        Sociology of Industrial Relations.** London:
        Routledge and Kegan Paul, 1981.

        Reviews various theories and empirical
research on trade unionism, and notes their
weaknesses. Develops a framework in which power
is a central explanatory variable. Looks at
various theories of power and emphasizes the
importance of distinguishing between power
resources and factors affecting the exercise of
power.
    A comprehensive review of the literature,
with a long bibliography.

361. Prandy, K., A. Stewart and R.M. Blackburn. **White Collar Unionism**. London: Macmillan, 1983.

     Complements the authors' book on white-collar work and is a further addition to the debate on the growth, nature and character of white-collar unionism. The claim is that issues of class cannot be explained solely by reference to the means of production. It is important "to look at the process of socially structured advantage and disadvantage, the ways in which these are reproduced and changed, and the consequences in terms of experience for groups differently located within the process."
     Although the claims put forward here has been criticized, a number of important questions relating to white-collar unionism are addressed.

362. Radice, G. **The Industrial Democrat: Trade Unions in an Uncertain World**, London: George Allen and Unwin, 1978.

     Examines the environment within which trade unions operate, and analyses their response to that environment. Suggests that trade unions need a strategy which takes into account the complexity of modern society in order to be able to represent and protect their members effectively, and that they move away from a defensive to a more positive approach. It also looks at the implications of this approach on trade union structure and services, and stresses the need for trade union involvement in the running of industry, along with a full recognition of their broad role.
     This is an important book, written by a labor M.P. and former union research officer, which makes a valuable contribution to the debate on industrial democracy.

     (A rejoinder to Items 352, 377)

363. Reshef, Y. and B. Bemmels. "Political and Economic Determinants of Strikes in Israel: A Sectoral Comparison." **Economic and Industrial Democracy**, 10(1) 1989, 35-57.

Examines strike activities among three sectors: the public, private and Histadrut (General Federation of Labour) in Israel between 1965 and 1984. Shows that economic determinants play a central role in the private sector, whereas political factors play a central part in the public and Histadrut sector.

A useful addition to the literature on strikes, and provides insights for comparative research.

364. Robinson, J.G. and J.S. McIlwee. "Obstacles to Unionization in High-tech Industries." **Work and Occupations,** 16(2) 1989, 115-136.

Attempts to answer the question, "Why is high-tech industry in the sunbelt so difficult to organize?" Locates the discussion within the theoretical debate regarding the decline of the unions in the United States. Finds the answer to the question in a combination of factors, such as employer resistance, work place disorganization and political climate.

An essential reading for issues related to obstacles to unionization and the decline of union membership.

365. Roxborough, I. **Unions and Politics in Mexico: The Case of the Automobile Industry.** Cambridge: Cambridge University Press, 1984.

Challenges 'the standard account' of the subordination of Mexican labor to state control. The division between militant and conservative unions proves to be a good predictor of differences, with respect to wages, job security and control of managerial prerogatives in the organization of work. Shows the differences between these two unions and concludes that union politics are complex and the rank and file in the plants manage to have an impact on union organizations.

Well-written study of industrial unionism in Mexico, and a useful source for those interested in the Latin American labor movement.

(A rejoinder to Items 341, 356)

366. Ruble, B.A. **Soviet Trade Unions: Their**
        Development in the 1970s. Cambridge:
        Cambridge University Press, 1981.

        Attempts to provide a complete portrait of
     union activity, both in the international and
     domestic arenas, and identifies several areas of
     continuity and change. Most changes are the result
     of pressure placed by current events on Marxist-
     Leninist theory; the process of adjusting this
     theory to reality has led to fundamental changes
     in union policies.
        Provides the basis for comparing Western
     trade unions with their Soviet counterparts. The
     long bibliography helps those interested to know
     more about collective bargaining in the Soviet
     Union.

     (A rejoinder to Item 378)

367. Sack, lJ. and T. Lee. "The Role of the State in
        Canadian Labour Relations." **Relations**
        Industriels, 44(1) 1989, 195-223.

        Canadian unions have been successful and the
     state has remained committed to the principle of
     collective bargaining. However, during the
     recessionary period, the state has wavered its
     intervention and eroded the collective bargaining
     rights.
        An important piece which helps to grasp the
     growing problems that unions have been facing in
     recent years.

     (A rejoinder to Item 352)

368. Smith, W. R. **Crisis in the French Labour**
        Movement: A Grassroots Perspective. New
        York: St. Martin's Press, 1987.

Examines the decline in union membership at
the local level and focuses on the activities of
shop stewards of the two major French unions, the
CGT and CFDT. Demonstrates that unions have not
sufficiently taken into account the changing
environment of the firm. Stresses the distance
that separates the shop stewards from the rank and
file. This explains in large part the lack of
control that French unions exert over strikes.

Rich in information and insights, and an
essential reading for students and activists
interested in the French labor movement.

369. Spalding, H.A. **Organized Labor in Latin America:
Historical Case Studies of Workers in
Dependent Societies.** New York: New York Univ.
Press, 1977.

Seeks to describe the advance of urban
organized labor in Latin America. Synthesizes
older and newer scholarships, and raises research
problems and areas for future investigation. Also
emphasizes the role that outside factors played in
Latin America's labor history, but does not deny
the importance of domestic events. Shows that
Latin American labor history displays a remarkable
unity, but that significant national differences
do exist, as well.

Records the persistent struggle of the Latin
American working class up to the mid-1960's. A
valuable addition to the study of Latin America's
labor history.

(A rejoinder to Items 341, 356, 370)

370. Southhall, R. (ed.). **Trade Unions and the New
Industrialization of the Third World,** London:
Zed Books Ltd., 1988.

Focuses on some of the major issues
confronting the world's trade unions today, and
shows that the globalization of production and the
prolonged recession in OECD countries, have
undermined the bargaining power of the unions.
Also looks at workers' responses to these new

challenges, and attempts to conceptualize the
contemporary tendencies on the world economy; i.e.
the new pattern of industrialization, the new
international division of labor and the new
capitalist accumulation process. Assesses the
implications of these new tendencies for capital
and labor.
   An excellent source for understanding the new
challenges which face Third World trade unions.

(A rejoinder to Item 369)

371. Southhall, R. "Migrants and Trade Unions in South
     Africa Today." **Canadian Journal of African
     Studies**, 20(2) 1986, 161-185.

   Rejects any notion that migrants are either
reluctant to join trade unions or are difficult to
organize. Migrants cannot be stereotyped, they
can only be understood as workers subject to
different pressures of the family, work place,
etc., raising varying responses in different
sociohistorical situations. We need to situate
different migrants into the class analysis of the
South African population.
   Of particular importance for its
categorization of various types of workers in
South Africa.

372. Streeck, W. **Industrial Relations in West Germany:
     A Case Study of the Car Industry**, New York,
     St. Martin's Press, 1984.

   Uses the case of the car industry to show why
trade unions continue to exist, and why they are
able to function and grow. Also analyses the
positive consequences of the legal
institutionalization of work place industrial
relations in Germany for the viability of
industrial unionism, showing that the trade
unions' influence on company policy is
institutionalized in the framework of industrial
democracy. How organizational structure,
institutionalized influence, and the responsible
behavior of trade unions are related, and how they

affect the use of manpower in industrial
production are also demonstrated.

This book is written with the aim of explaining
German industrial relations for those who are not
necessarily specialists in the field. It contains
a bibliography on German industrial relations in
English, for those who are interested in further
reading.

373. Swanson, D. "Annual Bibliography on American
        Labor History, 1986." **Labor History**, 28(4)
        1987, 484-496.

This annual publication uses a variety of
sources and provides a detailed bibliography on
American labor.

A rich source of information and a quick
introduction to the writings in the field.

374. Taylor, R. **Workers and the New Depression**.
        London: Macmillan, 1982.

Brings together and summarizes a
considerable amount of research on industrial
relations and labor economics that describe the
development. of the labor market. Challenges the
view that British trade unions have excessive
legal protection, but criticizes unions for
failing to achieve a greater degree of economic
equality for their members, especially the less
skilled. British unions are seen as displaying an
overwhelming desire to attain and maintain
privileges for themselves opposed to other groups
of workers. This leads to sectionalism,
compounded by multi-unionism and a weak central
control of local branches.

Shows the complex nature of the problems that
unions face. Makes an excellent complementary
text for British or comparative industrial
sociology.

375. Thompson, M., G. Swimmer(eds.). **Conflict or Compromise: The Future of Public Sector Industrial Relations**, Ottawa: the Institute for Research on Public Policy, 1984.

In recent years, collective bargaining for public employees has posed the most difficult challenge of policy facing governments. Shows the increase of collective bargaining in the public sector and discusses the conflictual nature of public unionism. On the one hand, it is believed that public servants' collective bargaining rights should be curtailed. On the other hand, public servants themselves think that government policies discriminately limit their rights.

Helps to better understand contemporary issues related to collective bargaining in the public sector.

(A rejoinder to Item 358)

376. Tomlins, C. L. **The State and the Unions: Labor Relations, Law and the Organized Labor Movement in America, 1880-1960.** Cambridge: Cambridge University Press, 1985.

Shows that in the first half century the AFL tried to limit the role of the government in its affairs. In the 1930's, the situation changed. Public figures believed that unions could play a constructive role in promoting economic development. Laborites embraced the state as a means of expanding union membership. Legalistic procedures made for a complex system of industrial relations. In the 1940's, the new law restricted the ability of the union to discuss the nature, content and organization of work. By the 1960's, the union was isolated into the role of a narrowly defined collective bargaining agent.

A provocative and impressive research which deserves a wide discussion and readership.

377. Von Beyme, K. **Challenge to Power: Trade Unions and Industrial Relations in Capitalist Countries.** Beverly Hills: Sage Publications, 1980.

    Attempts to develop a theory of trade union behavior as it is today, drawing evidence from practically all the countries of the industrial capitalist world. Among the issues discussed are: the failure of trade union movements to achieve solidarity; variations in union membership density; centralization and decentralization of union movements; the tension between various ideologies in the union; strike behavior and the effects of strikes; and the government's role in integrating unions into society.
    This is not an easy reading, but with its 933 citations, it represents a comprehensive assessment of research on union behavior.

    (A rejoinder to Items 352, 362)

378. Yanaev, G.I. "Soviet Restructuring: The Position and Role of the Trade Unions." **International Labour Review**, 126(6) 1987, 703-713.

    The Soviet Union has arrived at a major point in its history. It faces radical restructuring of its political, economic and cultural life. However, such a dramatic change will have far-reaching consequences for the Soviet trade union movement. It will face new challenges and must be equipped to handle new tasks as they arise.
    Raises important questions for understanding the issues facing the unions, and the economy as a whole in the Soviet Union.

    (A rejoinder to Item 366)

CHAPTER SIX

INDUSTRIAL DEMOCRACY
AND
ALTERNATIVE FORMS
OF ORGANIZATION

Industrial Democracy:
Alternative Forms of Organizations

379. Batstone, E., A. Ferner, and M. Terry. **Unions on the Board: An Experiment in Industrial Democracy.** Oxford: Basil Blackwell, 1983.

    Looks at the experiment of industrial democracy done on the Board of the Post Office in Britain. It has been the only attempt to test equal representation for unions and management at the corporate level. The authors consider the origin of the industrial democracy experiment, discuss the significance of the Board itself, look at the relationship between the unions and their nominees on the Board, and give a brief account of the termination of the industrial democracy experiment. More importantly, they draw a number of conclusions concerning the relevance of the experiment for the understanding of industrial democracy.
    A required book for students of industrial democracy.

380. Blyton, P. "Some Old and New Problems in Employee Participation in Decision-making." **International Social Science Journal**, 36(100) 1984, 217-232.

    With the development of industrialization, a number of important changes have occurred in patterns of management and structures of decision-making within enterprises. There has been a persistent interest in the participation of employees in organizational decision-making. Blyton critically looks at the development of employee participation and shows its limits. Suggests that for participation to develop more fully in the work place more emphasis must be put on the value of participation in society.
    Provides a comparative review of the development of participation and obstacles towards it.

381. Bradley, K. and A. Gelb. **Worker and Capitalism: The New Industrial Relations**. Cambridge: MIT Press, 1985.

    Through the decade of the 1980's, industrial policy in the western economies confronted subtle demands. To face the challenge, new forms of industrial policy were called for. Worker ownership was seen as a potentially superior alternative to government subsidies or protection. Calls for worker and workers' community ownership of business as a means of economic redevelopment. Makes observations based on case studies of employee ownership from the United States, Canada, France, and the United Kingdom.
    Provides valuable insights into the debate on industrial policy, and shows that employee ownership makes good economic sense. Useful for students of industrial relations and alternative forms of organizations.

382. Bradley, K. and A. Gelb. **Co-operative at Work, The Mondragon Experience**. London: Heinemann Educational Books, 1983.

    Mondragon, a network of co-operatives providing employment for over 18,000 members, with its own bank, its own technical school and its own social welfare agency, is located around the small town of Mondragon in the Basque region of Northern Spain. It has been successful and has outstripped the performance of the capitalist firms in the surrounding Basque economy. The authors ponder the possibility of successfully transplanting the experiment elsewhere and explore the secret of its success.
    Although the Mondragon co-operative comprises a single case and has limited generalizability, this is an important contribution and essential for those interested in alternative forms of work organization.

    (A rejoinder to Item 402)

383. Cuvillier, R. **The Reduction of Working Time.**
        Geneva: International Labour Organization,
        1984.

        Deals with the economic and social effects of
the reduction in working time in industrialized
market economies. Discusses the size of the
reduction in working time and gives general idea
about the scope of the reductions that are being
asked for. Concludes that large-scale reductions
in working time are needed to divide the work into
a larger number of jobs and recommends gradual
reductions with a forward-looking overall
structure in mind.
        Studies a subject which is, at present,
widely discussed and important to those interested
in alternative forms of organization.

        * *Ebel, K.H. (Item 238)*

384. Espinosa, J.G., and A.S. Zimbalist. **Economic
        Democracy: Workers' Participation in Chilean
        Industry 1970-1973.** New York: Academic Press,
        1981.

        The best examination of the complicated
process of enterprise democratization, and the
socioeconomic impact of increased worker
participation, in Chile during Allende's period.
It is based on an exhaustive analysis of the
literature in the field, which illustrates
politics at the grass roots. Also shows how the
Chilean working class increased its level of
participation, and why factory owners reacted so
violently.
        An impressive effort and a required reading
for anyone interested in workers' participation.

385. Euzeby, A. "Social Security and Part-time
        Employment." **International Labour Review,**
        127(5) 1988, 545-558.

        Reviews how part-time employment can be used
as a measure to help combat unemployment.

However, the existing security system, conceived
originally for full-time workers, is an obstacle
to such part-time work. Rapid technological
changes and growing international competition
require a more flexible working time. Part-time
employment is seen both as a form of work-sharing
and as means to satisfy the individual worker's
need.

Of great value to policy makers and those
interested in the study of future of work
organization.

(A rejoinder to Items 395, 398)

386. Gladstone, A.; R. Landsbury; J. Stieber; T. Treu
        and M. Weiss (eds.). **Current Issues in
        Labour Relations: An International
        Perspective**. New York: Walter de Gruyter,
        1989.

Discusses a number of important themes in
work place relations and managerial styles, as
they are being rethought and refashioned. New
trends in working-time arrangements and hours
worked in various countries have had much less
positive impact on employment than expected.
Brings a comparative dimension by dealing with co-
operation and conflict in public service labor
relations in various countries.

A valuable addition to the literature on
comparative study of new approaches to industrial
relations and the future of work.

387. Gramling, R. "Concentrated Work Scheduling:
        Enabling and Constraining Aspects."
        Sociological Perspective, 32(1) 1989, 47-64.

Discusses the relationship between the
interaction of time and space and human work
activities. Analyses the way in which technology
has lessened the constraint of time and space and
has fostered the pursuit of occupational and
economic goals. Modern technology, coupled with
flexible work scheduling has potential for

establishing flexible frontiers of both time and space.
A very useful addition to the discussion of the future of work.

* *Handy, C. (Item 93)*

388. Heller, F., P. Drenth, P. Koopman and V. Rus,
     **Decisions in Organizations: A Three Country
     Comparative Study**. London: Sage Publications,
     1988.

     Reviews the involvement of individuals and
     groups in the decision-making process.
     Theoretical and methodological issues are
     discussed in great detail, and some quantitative
     measures of the participation dynamics in the
     decision-making process are offered. Heller's
     attempt to qualify different dimensions of so many
     decisions in three different countries—the United
     Kingdom, the Netherlands, and Yugoslavia—is
     ambitious, stimulating and rich.
     A valuable source of information which
     invites discussion and offers a great number of
     suggestions to researchers.

* *Hirschhorn, L. (Item 243)*

389. International Labour Organization. **Workers'
     Participation in Decisions Within
     Undertakings**. Geneva: International Labour
     Organization, 1981.

     Expresses the views of the International
     Labour Organization and intends to provide up-to-
     date information on the various systems of
     workers' participation in decision-making in the
     private, mixed or public sectors. Covers
     developed and developing countries, the
     industrialized market economy and centrally
     planned economies.
     Can serve as a general introductory book on
     the topic, and is particularly useful for
     comparative purposes.

* *International Labour Organization (Item 53)*

390. Jain, H.C. **Worker Participation: Success and Problems**. New York: Praeger Publishers, 1980.

    Identifies the range and main features of participation in advanced industrialized countries and sets out the concept of worker participation in management. Reviews the literature and describes indirect forms of worker participation in supervisory and management boards in several western countries.
    Provides useful lessons from the western European experience, and indicates its relevance for practitioners, policy makers and researchers.

    * *Knight, D. (Item 57)*

391. Laaksonen, O. "Participation Down and Up the Line: Comparative Industrial Democracy Trends in China and Europe." **International Social Science Journal**, 36(100) 1984, 299-318.

    There have been many changes in enterprise management in China since the Cultural Revolution, including several attempts at participatory democracy. These systems are described, and their differences brought out. Discusses the new participation systems brought in after Chairman Maozedong's death and examines the influences of various interest groups in enterprises comparing them with European data.
    A must for students of labor relations in China.

392. Laflamme, G., L. Belanger, and M. Audet. "Workers' Participation and Personnel Policies in Canada: Some Hopeful Signs." **International Labour Review**, 126(2) 1987, 219-228.

    Since the early 1970's, a number of experiments in participation, ranging from profit-sharing to various forms of co-management and

self-management, have been tried in Canada. These
cases were initiated because of the recession. In
some cases workers have refused to allow the
closing down of their factories. In other cases
the supervisory staff have introduced profit-
sharing and employee shareholder schemes in order
to increase productivity.

A good overview of alternative forms of
organization.

393. Lindenfield, F. and J. Rothschild-Whitt (eds.).
     Work-place Democracy and Social Change.
     Boston: Porter Sargent Publishers, 1982.

     Challenges the claim that efficient and
     rational organization can be achieved only through
     highly bureaucratic means. Sheds light on the
     common characteristics of democratic work
     organizations, and the psychological impact of
     working in a democratically managed work
     organization. Discusses the implications of work
     place democracy for social change.

     Poses many important questions regarding
     organizational structure in democratic work
     places. Above all, provides an excellent summary
     of the writings and research in the area of work
     place democracy.

394. Luria,D.D. "New Labor-Management Models from
     Detroit." **Harvard Business Review,** 64(5)
     1986, 22.

     Surveys the United States auto industry, and
     examines the changes in work assignment and job
     classification rules and the trends in labor
     relations. Finds that the increasing competition
     forced the industry and union to negotiate a
     radically different type of contract. Rigid work
     rules are under attack, and multiple wage and
     benefit packages are chosen. Concludes that the
     co-operation between management and labor is
     crucial for the health and survival of the
     industry.

     Provides insights into trends in labor
     relations in manufacturing industries in the

United States, and into flexible work
organization.

395. Mangan, J. and J. Steinke. "Working Time
        Reduction in Australian Industry: Did they
        Create Jobs and Who Funded them?" **Economic
        and Industrial Democracy**, 9(2) 1988, 165-178.

    Investigates the relationship between
reductions in the length of the standard working
week, and employment and hourly wage costs, as
they emerged in Australia in 1976-1985. Raises
two main questions: whether working time
reductions reduced unemployment, and how work-time
changes were funded.
    Clarifies many of the issues currently
debated by those interested in alternative forms
of work.

(A rejoinder to Items 385, 398)

396. Nightingale, D.V. **Work-place Democracy: An
        Inquiry into Employee Participation in
        Canadian Organizations.** Toronto: University
        of Toronto Press, 1982.

Advocates the right of employees to participate in
organizational decision-making, as the natural
extension of the democratic entitlement found in
the political realm. Discusses two ideal types of
organizations: hierarchical and democratic. In
democratic organizations, conflict will be
resolved to reflect the greater common good. The
hierarchical organization is seen as out of date,
but the author does not investigate why work place
democracy is not the wave of the future.
    An important study which has a lot to offer
on the issue of power and profit sharing.

397. Poole, M. **Towards a New Industrial Democracy:
        Workers' Participation in Industry.** London:
        Routledge and Kegan Paul, 1986.

Elaborates on a new and broader understanding of industrial democracy by pulling together the various facets of direct and representative workers' participation, control and influence in industrial relations. Takes into account: Collective bargaining and other forms of union action; the new initiatives of managers; and the theoretical debate between evolutionary and cyclical schools on the long-term trends of the various manifestations of industrial democracy. Reminds the reader that workers' participation in decision-making may be best understood as one index of the exercise of power in industrial life.

A useful and informative book, well balanced by theoretical, historical and comparative discussions.

398. Ronen, S. **Flexible Working Hours: An Innovation in the Quality of Work Life.** New York: McGraw-Hill Book Co., 1981.

Uses an organizational, psychological approach to the study of a flexible time system. Takes examples from both private and public sectors to analyze a wide variety of topics, and presents a summary of the advantages and disadvantages of flexible time to employers, employees and society. Relates flexible working hours to the special problems of commuters, women workers, supervisors and unions. Reviews problems associated with the implementation of flexible working time.

Contains a large number of useful references, and deals with a topic of utmost importance in the contemporary world of work.

(A rejoinder to Items 385, 395)

399. Rus, V. "The Future of Industrial Democracy." **International Social Science Journal,** 36(100) 1984, 233-257.

Takes the risk of dealing with industrial democracy forecasting and postulates a number of theses. Sees very few countries in which

industrial democracy could be promoted by
legislation, but indicates there are better
chances to develop industrial democracy at the
micro-level of daily work if certain conditions
are present.
     Brings out some of the factors which impede
or promote the development of industrial
democracy. A valuable addition to the literature
in the field.

400. Schwarz, R.M. "Participative Decision Making:
         Comparing Union Management-Designed Incentive
         Pay Programs." **Group and Organization
         Studies**, 14(1) 1989, 104-122.

     This study is based on the surveys of two
sites with participatory decision-making programs
designed solely by the management. Suggests that
the first programs were more equitable, more
motivating and generated higher level of
satisfaction than the latter programs.
     A useful piece for managers, consultants and
others concerned with participative decision-
making.

     * *Shirley, S. (Item 118)*

401. Spinard, W. "Work Democracy: An Overview."
         International Social Science Journal, 36(100)
         1984, 195-216.

     Democratizing work organizations has had its
passionate proponents. Precise efforts at
achieving some types of work democracy have become
more prominent since the post World War period,
especially in the western world. Spinard
considers some of the motivations behind these
attempts and makes a number of observations which
serve as a guide in helping to further the
objectives of work democracy.
     A clear description of what actually happened
and what could happen regarding work place
democracy.

402. Thornley, J. **Workers' Co-operatives: Jobs and Dream**. London: Heinemann Educational Books, 1981.

Compares workers' co-operatives in Britain with those in France and Italy to find out why they are weak and small in comparison. The problems are seen as being internal to the workers' co-operatives and their supporters. Outlines the development of the ideas behind the workers' co-operatives from the 19th century, and examines the weaknesses of the capital structure of co-operatives. The utopian drive behind co-operatives is suggested to have seriously hindered their growth.
It is doubtful that Thornley has succeeded to relates weaknesses of workers' co-operatives in Britain to a particular pattern of industrial development, but she offers useful information on the co-operatives.

(A rejoinder to Item 382)

403. White, R.D. **Law, Capitalism and the Right to Work**. Toronto: Garmond Press, 1986.

Provides a critical discussion of how workers' rights are dealt with in the Canadian legal system and documents how specific pieces of legislation affect unionists and women. Makes a strong case for the need to recognize social rights, and evaluates the limitations and negative features of the current Canadian economic and political system.
While limited in scope, addresses many issues common to labour law in industrialized countries.

* *Wilkes, J. (Item 127)*

404. Witte, J.F. **Democracy, Authority and Alienation in Work: Workers' Participation in an American Corporation**. Chicago: The University of Chicago Press, 1980.

Addresses issues relating to workers' belief in participation, problems confronting decision-making, and conflict between democracy and meritocracy. The case used is an American electronics manufacturing firm which attempted to engage workers in various levels of decision-making. The information comes from interviews, company statistics, observation and tape analysis.

A well documented case study and a welcome addition to the literature on industrial democracy.

405. Wolfe, J.D. **Workers, Participation, and Democracy**. Westport, Ct.: Greenwood Press, 1985.

Examines if participatory democracy is possible in large-scale union and party organization. Focuses on the internal politics of the British trade union during the first World War and shows that during this period rank-and-file members controlled the decision-making process and set the agenda. Emphasizes the growing role of the shop steward to demonstrate the existence of participatory democracy in class conscious workshops.

Although criticized on a number of grounds, it provides insightful discussion on workers' participation in decision-making.

INDEXES

AUTHOR INDEX

SUBJECT INDEX

For Product Safety Concerns and Information please contact our EU
representative GPSR@taylorandfrancis.com Taylor & Francis Verlag GmbH,
Kaufingerstraße 24, 80331 München, Germany

Printed and bound by CPI Group (UK) Ltd, Croydon, CR0 4YY
01/05/2025
01858443-0001